This book is due for return on or before the last date shown below.

The Young Audience:
Exploring and Enhancing Children's Experiences of Theatre

Matthew Reason

A Trentham Book
Institute of Education Press, London

Institute of Education Press
20 Bedford Way
London
WC1H 0AL

First published 2010

British Library Cataloguing-in-Publication Data
A catalogue record for this book is available from the
British Library

Cover illustration features drawings by Ajay, Ben, Isha, Karen,
Lorraine, Mantas and Megan

ISBN 978 1 85856 450 0

Printed by CPI Group (UK) Ltd, Croydon, CR0 4YY

Contents

Dedication

For Alison

Acknowledgements

My sincere thanks to Alice McGrath, Tony Reekie and Imaginate for their co-operation and involvement with many stages of this project. I would also like to thank all the children, teachers and schools who participated in the research for making the project so rewarding and exciting.

Thanks for allowing me to reproduce their words or images to Philip Pullman, Tony Graham, Peter Manscher and Peter Jankovic, and Lisa Barnard. I would also like to thank Morag MacInness, Alison Reeves and Brian Hartley who facilitated the research workshops in various ways.

I am extremely grateful to the Scottish Government Education Department for financial support for the initial stages of the research.

Finally, I would like to thank my partner Alison Dyke and acknowledge the role of my own children – Nathaniel and Aidan – in enhancing my own engagement in theatre for children and young people.

Introduction

Theatre for children, that is theatre written, directed and produced specifically for young audiences, is enjoying a period of thriving activity and interest in the UK. This is demonstrated by more targeted funding support, the prestige gained by certain children's theatre companies, and the vastly increased attention being paid to questions of quality. Once something of a Cinderella, much neglected in comparison with theatre for grown-ups, theatre for children in the UK has now gained a level of respect and attention like that traditionally accorded children's theatre in Europe and the United States.

The growth in the status of theatre for children as an art form has been accompanied by widespread interest in the social and educational benefits for young people of the arts in general and theatre in particular. Yet there has been almost no reflective research into this area. While young children (aged 4-11) are increasingly provided for in terms of tailored theatre performances, children's perceptions of theatre and their audience experiences have scarcely been investigated. Although there is research on the relationship between the arts and education, there is little that deals with children's engagement with theatre as theatre. In the clamour of voices advocating the importance of theatre for young people, the voice and the perspective of the children themselves is missing.

It is this gap that *The Young Audience* sets out to fill, using original qualitative audience research to uncover the nature of young children's experiences of live theatre. This book provides a resource for teachers, artists, researchers, students, policy makers and other professionals working with theatre and children, in a range of contexts and environments. It enhances existing cultural policy and educational understandings of theatre for children by providing detailed, analytical and methodologically grounded insight into how young children perceive and respond to live theatre performances.

Not just why and what, but also how

When thinking about theatre for children, two kinds of questions that are generally posed ask either: *why* should children watch theatre? Or *what* kind of theatre should children watch?

The thoughts implied by the question 'why should children experience theatre?' are somewhat pernicious. There is an off-hand, but entirely understandable desire to respond with a pithy 'why not?' Another equally valid response might be to say, 'for all the reasons adults should experience theatre.' Like many pithy and pointed answers, these have an element of truth about them: does theatre for children really need to continually assert specific justifications for its very existence? For those with a commitment to delivering and supporting theatre for children and young people, the why question is almost redundant. As Tony Reekie, chief executive of the Imaginate in Edinburgh, puts it:

> I think generally you have to go, can we just take it as a given? That if children have got access to art and culture in its broadest sense, it is actually a good thing. (personal interview, 2006)

This perception is passionately advocated by Philip Pullman in his manifesto stating the importance of 'Theatre – the true key stage'. An extract is reproduced later in this book. Pullman writes that 'Children need to go to the theatre as much as they need to run about in the fresh air' and continues:

> I'm not going to argue about this: I'm right. Children need art and music and literature; they need to go to art galleries and museums and theatres; they need to learn to play musical instruments and to act and to dance. They need these things so much that human rights legislation alone should ensure that they get them. (Pullman, 2004)

Why should children watch theatre? Because, as Pullman suggests, if they do not 'they perish on the inside'? Because, as asserted by Reekie, it is good for them? At one level such perceptions are not dissimilar to those around theatre for adults, which we often unconsciously position as good for us, often contrasting it with supposedly less worthy or more harmful engagement with popular culture or television. Such assertions contain implicit perceptions – about value, quality, benefit, childhood – that warrant further consideration.

Is *all* theatre good for children, simply because it is theatre? Can theatre really be a right in the same way as shelter and kindness are defined as the universal rights of a child? Is it ever possible to think of theatre for children as *theatre* and outside of educational agendas? These questions are pertinent because it is adults who have the power in this relationship and who make the judgements about what is good for children. Although tempting to take such debates as resolved, there are still too many implied questions and value judgements.

In 1961, Kenneth Graham outlined five positive values of engaging children with theatre, which by and large still predominate in cultural discourses today. These were: entertainment, psychological growth, educational exposure, aesthetic appreciation and the development of a future audience (cited in Goldberg, 1974:14). Although grouped and described differently in contemporary discourses, these five elements continue to represent the 'good things' that come of engaging children with theatre and it is largely these concerns that are developed in the early chapters of this book, which consider the educational, policy and artistic contexts that impact on the production of theatre for children.

Within each of these contexts, theatre for children becomes a different entity: shaped, defined, supported and evaluated according to overlapping but distinct criteria. Within each context, however, some of the same fundamental questions recur. Chapter One opens this discussion by exploring the relationship between theatre for children and education. Education is a dominant theme in this context, a prime motivator for the production of theatre for children that at the same time has the potential to stifle and restrict what is made and how it is perceived. In Chapter Two the discussion broadens to consider further key discourses surrounding theatre for children in terms of audience development, cultural habitus and cultural rights. Ending this section, Chapter Three considers the ways in which quality in theatre for children can be conceptualised in terms of the ambitions that are held for its audience. Interspaced between the chapters you will find commentaries, manifestos and perspectives from Philip Pullman, Tony Graham and Peter Manscher.

Part One thus presents the vital contextualising ground to the book's primary ambition, which is to go beyond the familiar questions of *why* children should experience theatre, and of *what* kind, and instead examine *how* children watch, understand, engage with and remember theatre.

Drawing the theatrical experience

What do children remember and talk about after a theatre performance? What kinds of things do they value, consider important or forget? What theatrical competences and interpretative strategies do they bring to the task of watching a performance? How do children identify and construct narrative or character? How do children interact within an audience? What levels of illusion and reality do young children perceive in theatrical performances?

These were some of the questions I started with in a project entitled 'Drawing the Theatrical Experience', which took place in 2007 in collaboration with Imaginate. The project's sub-title, 'How do children watch theatre?' accurately described our objectives, but was perhaps overly ambitious in its simplicity. Different children watch different performances in very different ways and the exact nature of the experience remains to a huge extent private – how children watch theatre, taken literally, is an impossible question. With these caveats in mind, I conducted detailed qualitative audience research with young children for this project, using participative arts-based workshops as a central methodological tool, so as to listen closely to what children had to say about their experiences.

This material forms the bulk of the middle section of this book. Part Two: The Theatrical Experience explores children's experiences of theatre, with chapters considering the relationship between experience and the imagination; young children's theatrical competence; and children's engagement with theatre on moral or metaphorical levels. These discussions bring to the fore and contemplate the private act of watching theatre. This book *about* children watching theatre also features Lisa Barnard's striking photographs *of* children watching theatre.

In their rich and detailed account of children's experience of watching theatre, these chapters follow ethnographic traditions of research and provide unique evidence of how children perceive and respond to live theatre performances. Part Two unpicks and explores the methodologies used in gathering the data, partly because this inevitably influences the kinds of material collected and the stories told, but also because the methodology became itself a result of the research.

Extending engagement

The workshops conducted within the 'Drawing the Theatrical Experience' project were intended to be fun and rewarding for the children who took part, as well as useful in research terms. At the very least they would have a good time making pictures for people who were interested in what they drew and what they said. While aware that all research activity changes the nature of that which it is observing, what I did not explicitly anticipate was that this methodological approach would also positively affect the children's theatrical experiences. This is what happened, however: during the workshops it became apparent that the process of drawing and talking gave the children the chance to reflect upon, develop and deepen their engagement.

The chapters in Part Three: Extending Engagement develop this insight, exploring what kinds of afterlife a performance has in a child's memory, how this afterlife might be extended, and how children actively play with their experiences after the event. This section is founded upon the understanding that engaging children with theatre involves more than simply sitting them down in front of a production. It involves a responsibility to contextualise the experience and provide the audience with skills of spectatorship. So these chapters are toolboxes, intended to help guide the deepening of children's experiences and also to continue philosophical discussions about the nature of artistic engagement. Part Three is aimed particularly at artists, researchers, students and teachers who need to engage young children in dialogue about their artistic and theatre experiences.

The positions of artist, teacher and researcher are conflated in the book, as all are seen as engaged in aesthetic enquiry with children and all as possessing various kinds of knowledge about the nature of children's theatrical experience. I hope the book will provide a useful resource for all these people and for others who work with theatre and with children in a range of contexts and environments. I hope also that it will help refocus attention on the young audience's experience of theatre.

Part One
Contexts and Questions

1
Theatre for Children and Education

The relationship between young people and the arts is rarely perceived as simply a matter of enjoyment. It is almost always about something else too. Often that something is the learning, the education, the benefit (or harm) children might gain from the experience. But then all aspects of young children's play and socialising, as well as their formal education, form part of their ongoing developmental engagement with the world. As Martin Buber observes, '*everything* educates', everything makes an impression and gives form to experiences (cited in Bresler and Thompson, 2002:9).

For most children, this learning development through rich encounters with the world happens instinctively and does not need to be made intentional or overt. Many adults, however, have a wish to make this learning explicit and to turn it into formalised education and schooling. It is interesting that many scholars have traced a link between the development of the theatre for children movement in the 1920s and 30s and the rise in the early 20th century of the concept of childhood itself. In his influential book *Centuries of Childhood* (1979), Philippe Ariès traces this invention of a 'myth' of childhood, central motifs of which include innocence, vulnerability and the need for protection and nurturing in the formative, educational years. As childhood became constructed as a particular stage in our development as people, so too did it become a stage associated with and identified by education and learning. This also has particular class and labour connotations. Andrea Gronemeyer, for example, notes that the rise of the middle-class 'brought with it an interest in instructive children's theatre' (cited in Schonmann, 2006:35).

Theatre for children has therefore always existed in overlapping frames of reference, evoking discourses of education as much as aesthetics; of pedagogy as much as art. In this it is different from theatre for adults, which might be valued for its enlightening or edifying characteristics but is rarely centrally perceived as educational. There are of course exceptions, but discussion about adult theatre is almost always discussion about aesthetics, art and theatre. Discussion about theatre for children is rarely so straightforward and is as often about education as about art.

Framed by this perception, this chapter sets out to map contemporary relationships, practices, contexts and issues, exploring the various ways in which theatre for children connects with and exists within discourses and practices of education.

Theatre and education: Theatre in Education

Attempts to demark territories and establish firm definitions can be dry and frustrating. However, it is worth discussing the distinction between theatre for children – that is professional theatre performances for young audiences – and Theatre in Education (TiE). Both are forms of theatre for children and both often exist and operate within systems of education, yet there are important distinctions that are useful to discuss when thinking about the relationship between theatre and education.

TiE in the United Kingdom is a fairly firmly identifiable movement, which originated in the 1960s and is concerned with the use of theatre as a method of education. There are many different routes and practices within TiE, but fundamental to many of these would be a programme of activity that might include a theatrical performance but would also encompass other participative elements including workshops, talks, playback and the use of forum theatre. For Tony Jackson it is this programme of activity that 'distinguishes TiE most obviously from other kinds of young people's theatre':

> The TiE programme is not a performance in schools of a self-contained play, a 'one-off' event that is here today and gone tomorrow, but a co-ordinated and carefully structured pattern of activities, usually devised and researched by the company, around a topic of relevance both to the school curriculum and to the children's own lives, presented in school by the company and involving the children directly in an experience of the situations and problems that the topic throws up. (1993:4)

Chris Vine echoes this description when he writes that TiE's 'prime motivation lies in its explicit educational purpose and that its distinctive formal feature is its use of active audience participation' (1993:109). There are, therefore, two principal elements at play within the concept of TiE that distinguish it from theatre for children. The first concerns the position of education as the primary motivation and function. In contrast, while theatre for children inevitably operates within contexts of education and learning, this is less frequently presented as its primary function. The second concerns this participatory process, or programme of activities, which is central to TiE but contrasted to the one-off nature of the professional performance.

Writing in 1993, Jackson notes that changes in the political climate in the UK, combined with funding pressures, have meant that since the 1980s there has been a shift away from participative programmes to performance only pieces (1993:23), a process that has largely continued in recent years. It is worth noting that professional children's theatre companies have increasingly sought to provide schools with study guides and packs that seek to facilitate teachers in preparing children for the performance and leading discussions or activities afterwards. These two factors have perhaps increasingly brought TiE and theatre for children closer together, a process already in evidence in the 1990s when Lowell Swortzell observed 'what was once TiE's exclusive terrain is now increasingly and highly effectively encroached upon by professional companies for young people' (1993:241).

Today in particular, therefore, it is increasingly difficult to construct firm distinctions between TiE and theatre for children in each of its different forms. One strong distinction, however, may be found in the instrumental motivation of much TiE and in the particular relationship that each form seeks to construct with education.

TiE, for instance, has often sought to construct fairly direct links between content and either academic or 'life skills' aspects of the curriculum. TiE programmes can typically be identified by subject focus: the last days of the British Raj; the Chartist Movement; racism in the 1930s. In doing so, TiE utilises the ability of theatre to make connections with subject areas in the humanities and sciences. Indeed, the effectiveness of theatre as a way of communicating the principles and practices of scientific thinking continues to be widely recognised (Bennett, 2005:23). Similarly, TiE uses theatre practices and processes to support learning in areas of personal, social and health education, and in the newer areas of citizenship and environmental studies, with productions and activities designed to increase awareness of the issues, stimulate empathy and encourage self-reflection and development.

In each of these areas, theatre is seen as an effective and fun method of communicating ideas and information. Indeed, the effectiveness of theatre is such that in the United Kingdom, while not routinely provided as a subject in its own right in primary schools, theatre is frequently used to facilitate the delivery of other subjects across the entire curriculum.

Almost since its inception, however, such programmes have been accompanied by questions and confusion over the relationship within TiE between theatre and education, and particularly the criticism that in serving education theatrical quality has been sacrificed. Writing as far back as 1974, for example, Sara Spencer observed from an American perspective that, 'while in general I found [TiE in England] rich and exciting and contemporary, in my judgement the scripting was often of poor quality, scenery scuffed, costumes grubby. TiE has many values. I would just hope that our children would not grow up to think this was theatre!' (cited in Swortzell, 1993:240).

Tony Jackson rightly points out that such criticism can lead to a flawed argument that asks 'education or theatre?', positioning the two as an incompatible dichotomy. In answering this complaint Jackson quotes Bertolt Brecht:

> 'Generally there is felt to be a very sharp distinction between learning and amusing oneself. The first may be useful, but only the second is pleasant. ... Well, all that can be said is that the contrast between learning and amusing oneself is not laid down by divine rule ... Theatre remains theatre, even when it is instructive, and in so far as it is good theatre it will amuse.' (cited in Jackson, 1993:34)

This may well be so, but in the context of theatre for children I also have sympathy with the argument that, while theatre certainly is a powerful medium for learning, this works best when it is theatre at its best. The particular consideration of what this might mean can be postponed until Chapter Three, which deals directly with the question of 'quality'. Here, however, it is worth examining in closer detail some of the arguments about TiE and theatre for children.

The arts and academic achievement

TiE has traditionally been fairly educationally directed, making explicit connections with areas of curricula or social development. The suggestion, in short, is that TiE is an effective vehicle through which to deliver learning. At the same time, TiE has also articulated its benefits in terms of the less formal education of 'the whole child'. While the discursive framework in which such claims are made is fairly strong and persuasive, there is far less available in the way of hard evidence.

This is in part because it is difficult to measure or quantify the direct and attributable benefits of arts engagement, particularly if any firm causal claims are being made. For example, in the UK the National Foundation for Education Research (NFER) enquiry into the effectiveness of arts education in secondary schools (no comparable research into primary schools exists) strikes a range of cautionary notes, stating that often the arts only register an effect on the most committed of pupils and that parental interest and support remains the single most significant factor in terms of young people's engagement with the arts (Harland *et al*, 2000).

However, bearing in mind such cautions, the argument that the arts in general and, not insignificantly, theatre within the arts, can play a role in delivering a whole range of informal educational benefits – such as enhancing creativity, communication, personal development, developing communication skills and increased overall achievements – is being increasingly supported by research in this area. The NFER, for example, asserts the 'impressive array of outcomes' registered in pupils taking the arts. These include:

- a heightened sense of enjoyment, excitement, fulfilment and therapeutic release of tensions

- an increase in the knowledge and skills associated with particular art forms

- enhanced knowledge of social and cultural issues

- the development of creativity and thinking skills

- the enrichment of communication and expressive skills

- advances in personal and social development

- effects that transfer to other contexts, such as learning in other subjects

- the world of work and cultural activities outside of school
  (Harland *et al*, 2000:565)

In their summary statement, the authors cite the 'vivid testimonies' of pupils and teachers asserting these and other benefits and conclude that, 'the range of outcomes associated with strong arts provision was wider than that codified in the National Curriculum and broader than the current focus on creative and cultural education' (Harland *et al*, 2000:566). Similarly, in a review of research literature into the expressive arts in education, carried out by the University of Strathclyde, the authors note that 'the findings of numerous, wide-ranging studies indicate that the Expressive Arts fulfil a vital function in the development of learners' (McNaughton *et al*, 2003:4).

Similar conclusions have been reached outside the UK, with one of the clearest articulations coming from the United States in a 1999 report entitled *Champions of Change* that brought together the work of a number of researchers exploring the impact of the arts on learning. The executive summary for the *Champions of Change* report states:

> When well taught the arts provide young people with authentic learning experiences that engage their minds, hearts, and bodies. The learning experiences are rich and meaningful to them.
>
> While learning in other disciplines may often focus on development of a single skill of talent, the arts regularly engage multiple skills and abilities. Engagement in the arts [...] nurtures the development of cognitive, social, and personal competencies. (Fiske, 1999:ix)

Amongst the material collected within the *Champions of Change* report is a statistical analysis by Catterall, Chapleau and Iwanaga exploring the inter-relationships between arts participation or attendance and academic achievement. This research suggested that pupils with high levels of arts engagement consistently outperformed 'arts poor' students, with the gap increasing over time. In itself this is not surprising for, as the research notes, the probability of being 'arts rich' is twice as high for students from economically advantaged families, while the probably of being 'arts poor' is twice as high for students from economically disadvantaged families (Catterall *et al*, 1999: 7). In other words, levels of children's arts engagement tend to match that of their parents, a theme explored further in Chapter Two.

However, Catterall, Chapleau and Iwanaga's research also specifically looked at the impact that high and low levels of arts engagement had on children from low socio-economic status backgrounds. Here the patterns of positive academic development for children engaged in the arts also applied to children from low socio-economic status backgrounds (Catterall *et al*, 1999:2). There are, therefore, reasonable grounds to suggest a statistical correlation between arts engagement and academic achievement. As the researchers noted, this correlation serves to emphasise the unfairness of unequal arts access amongst children.

As another paper in the *Champions of Change* report entitled 'Learning in and through the arts' describes:

> The researchers found that young people in 'high arts' groups performed better than those in low-arts groups on measures of creativity, fluency, originality, elaboration and resistance to closure – capacities central to arts learning.

> Pupils in arts-intensive settings were also strong in their abilities to express thoughts and ideas, exercise their imaginations and take risks in learning. (Burton *et al*, 1999:36)

Most of the research in this area examines the arts experiences of secondary school children. There is no reason to believe, however, that similar arguments would not be justified in a primary school context, not least because here the boundary between formal and informal education is less distinct and the arts and active learning techniques have even more of a presence. One recent piece of research in this area was a survey on the role and value of the arts in primary schools in England, carried out in 2003 by the National Foundation for Educational Research. In terms of the perceptions of headteachers and class teachers of the purposes of arts education in schools, one of the NFER's primary findings was that:

> The most highly endorsed purposes for the teaching of the arts were to develop creative and thinking skills and to develop communication and expressive skills. These were followed by purposes associated specifically with learning in the arts. [...] Headteachers produced testimonies to the contribution that the arts can make to motivation, behaviour, attendance and self-esteem, and many headteachers viewed the arts as central to raising standards in school. (Downing *et al*, 2003:19)

Headteacher and teacher support for the arts in primary education is particularly strong in terms of what is described as the importance of the arts in developing the 'whole child'; a concept related to broadening horizons, challenging expectations, providing new experiences and developing life skills and confidence. As remarks by one headteacher puts it, the arts allow children to

> get a different worldview, perhaps going from being a very narrow one to a very wide one. They see aesthetic quality, where they wouldn't have seen aesthetic quality before. The increased worldview gives them higher expectations and higher confidence. (Downing *et al*, 2003:15)

Indeed, the strength of support for arts education from within the primary school sector affirms a remark in a piece of research entitled 'Delivering the Arts in Scottish Schools' that suggested 'schools emerged as something of a stronghold for the arts – teachers saw schools as valuing the arts more than parents or the nation as a whole' (Wilson *et al*, 2005:5 and 59). In other words, the benefit that the arts can play in a child's education, which is being slowly confirmed by research, is something that has been widely claimed, intuitively and persuasively, by those working with children either as teachers or as theatre practitioners.

Similar perceptions are articulated from within the theatre industry. For example, Martin Drury asserts that 'if children have poor or limited arts experiences then their selves are poorer and more limited than would be otherwise the case' (2006:151). Within the arts such perceptions have been adopted as a potent discursive tool in cultural policy debates. Through this discourse the arts have laid claim to a particularly powerful position in terms of their ability to engage young people's imaginative and creative abilities. The claim is that theatre and the arts have a central role in enabling an educational approach that is creativity centred and thereby enhances children's capacities for learning across a range of formal and informal areas.

Learning in the arts

The perception stressed by the various reports and research explored above can be summarised as focusing on the possibilities of learning *through* the arts. That is, learning that is enhanced or delivered through using the arts as a tool that is utilised because of its instrumental effectiveness in aiding learning, rather than any desire to engage children with art for its own sake. Indeed, far less attention is paid to what could be described as learning *in the arts*, which might include specific art form skills and knowledge. Here, learning is not directed towards something outside the form itself, but instead concerns the nature of the individual's artistic experiences.

In one piece of research conducted by the NFER, headteachers and teachers were asked to respond to a pre-set list of 'purposes' for teaching the arts in schools. In their responses, the third most frequently cited purpose that teachers provided for teaching the arts in schools, not far behind 'creative and thinking skills' and 'communication and expressive skills', was 'pleasure'. This is underplayed by the NFER's analysis – it is not mentioned in the executive summary – but is surely significant. The NFER's disregard of pleasure is perhaps indicative of a wider focus on the educational or social uses of theatre, rather than theatre as art and as *experience*.

An emphasis on pleasure would suggest that the relationship between education and theatre within primary schools should focus on exploration of the art form in its own right. The reward of watching theatre, in other words, can often be located in the act of watching rather than in something to be extracted from the experience. Such learning in the arts is something that has been increasingly stressed by the education departments of children's theatre companies and can be thought of as the result of a move away from TiE and directly curriculum focused activity. Cecily O'Neill, for example, working with the Unicorn Theatre's Education Department, writes that

> At the same time as helping children towards an understanding of how theatre is made, the programme aims to encourage active engagement with artists, participation in some of the fundamental processes and practices of theatre and exploration of ways of interpreting and representing dramatic experience. (2005:11)

In another NFER report, *Saving a Place for the Arts*, it is suggested that theatre is the arts subject, particularly in comparison to music and the visual arts, taught least frequently as a lesson in its own right. It was also the arts subject least likely to be included in Initial Teacher Training and the most neglected in Continuing Professional Development. At the same time it was the subject most widely used in cross-curricular teaching and the most widely offered as an after school activity. The NFER also notes that schools make more use of theatre companies than any other outside professional arts organisation (Downing *et al*, 2003:37-49).

Extrapolation from these fairly contradictory indicators can only be speculative. However, one suggestion would be that theatre is perceived at policy level as a subject requiring low specialism from teachers, particularly in contrast to music, but with widely diverse application and appeal. That this is combined with the high levels of investment in outside expertise is intriguing, suggesting that the need for greater specialism is recognised at local and school levels.

Connected to this is the concern that while some teachers are well able to support arts education, the low levels of specialist theatre skills and expertise amongst teachers means that this is not true of all of them. One of the primary findings of research into delivering the arts in schools was that many teachers had a 'lack of confidence in teaching one or more areas of the expressive arts' (Wilson *et al*, 2005:4). Knowledge, confidence and interest are essential in teaching arts subjects. A lack of these qualities inhibits teachers' ability to deliver the contextualising and follow-up activities that so enrich children's experiences of performances. As Tony Reekie states, 'I think fundamentally you have a situation where teachers aren't comfortable with the arts. It is not part of what they do. Not part of their training. To expect them to work with and interpret something is then difficult' (personal interview, 2006).

This perception that many teachers are not entirely confident with the arts, with neither specialist training nor personal experience, has prompted Reekie to lead Imaginate in working with teachers, developing learning partnerships with schools and the education sector designed to improve skills and broaden perceptions. This investment in high quality professional development for teachers designed to broaden their understanding and experience of the arts now forms one of Imaginate's main areas of activity, alongside their programming of theatre for children during the Imaginate Festival. Training and developing the teachers, rather than using outside specialists, is strongly recommended by researchers. They stress the need for all teachers to be able to deliver the full curriculum in primary schools (Wilson *et al*, 2005:57). The importance of confident art teachers is affirmed by research that asserts that factors such as teacher influence are probably the most important, compared to whole school factors for example, in terms of the effectiveness of arts education in schools (Harland *et al*, 2000:569).

This chapter has suggested that the support structures surrounding children's engagement with the arts are often as vital as the art form experience itself. In this context the levels of teacher experience and confidence are key to the successful delivery of theatre education – practical suggestions for support in this area are described in Part Three of this book.

Theatre as education

The exploration in this chapter of the perceived educational and developmental benefits of theatre for children and young people has not set out to prove or measure these benefits. Instead it has been primarily interested in describing the policy discourses and debates that frame children's theatre provision and present contexts against which to explore the empirical research data presented later in this book.

While the specific debates and arguments within these policy discourses are nuanced, there is almost inevitably at some point a shift from such complexities to what is a more ingrained and culturally cherished perception of the inherent value of the arts. Broadly speaking, this is the perception that the arts – theatre, music, painting and so on – have value in a child's development beyond its immediate instrumental function and beyond anything that might be empirically demonstrated. This is the perception that engagement with the arts is a 'good thing', something that should be fostered without the need for concrete, measurable evidence.

Described as a 'good thing', engagement with the arts seems to be invested with not just educational benefit but also moral and health giving benefit as well – good for you in the same manner as daily prayer or an apple a day is good for you. There are dangers here that such perceptions are based as much upon class and upbringing as upon evidence and opportunity. There is also a danger that, in discussing the good that theatre for children might do, we fail to discuss whether theatre for children is itself good or not. This aesthetic perspective, the engagement with theatre as art and for pleasure, is often neglected in considering all the other good things theatre might do – although the real danger is that without being good in its own right theatre may not be able to do good at all.

Such is the embedding of theatre for children within discourses of education and instrumentalism that Shifra Schonmann rails against the 'tyranny of the didactic uses of children's theatre' and declares that

> It has to stop struggling to define its legitimacy as an educational endeavour, it would do better to concentrate on its artistic form and its own aesthetic merits (2006:10)

This is in many ways a laudable manifesto and one, moreover, that would be echoed across much of the children's theatre industry today. However, theatre for children *does* exist within the overlapping spheres of education and theatre – not least because almost all children's activity, right or wrongly, tends to be considered at least partly through the prism of education. Schonmann's statement raises questions about aesthetic merit and about whether with theatre for children education and art can be entirely untangled.

It is, however, easy to see how the association of theatre with schools and education has the potential to leave certain enduring negative associations in the minds of some children, particularly as they grow older. If theatre is heavily subsumed into an educational agenda, this can mitigate against other aspects of the experience. Such activities can become artificial experiences, not entirely satisfactory to anybody. John Tulloch, for example, draws from his own research with secondary school audiences the conclusion that 'the students rarely come away from the formal performance of the play separate, as it were, from their 'A-level' reading of it' (2000:98) and that it is often difficult to get young people to talk about theatre in a way that is not 'inevitably associated with the 'formal curriculum'' (2000:104). Jeanne Klein makes a similar point in the American context, suggesting that we need to consider seriously the possibility that 'we are raising generations of spectators who perceive theatre as an incomprehensibly abstract medium intended primarily for school field trips' (2005:53). As Ken Robinson puts it in the *All Our Futures* report on creative and cultural education:

> the term education is sometimes unhelpful. It can carry connotations of worthiness and civic duty which feel at odds for some artists with the excitement that drives them. If the term education prompts a listless commitment it should be dropped. (2001:132)

Interestingly, the movement away from TiE as a directly educational tool, to theatre for children as a more essentially artistic form, is potentially radical in this context. Theatre for children is in some ways more ambiguous in terms of the good it can do, which paradoxically means that the claims it must make are suddenly more ambitious. Unable to make small but specific claims about enhancing specific areas of the curriculum, children's theatre makes grandiose claims about enriching the soul. American youth theatre director Peter Brosius' comments are perhaps typical:

> We make theater to help our audience see that the world is knowable, malleable and demands critical thinking. We make theater so that young people will realize that there is tremendous power in their imagination. If they embrace that power, they can change the world. (2001:75)

For Moses Goldberg, theatre for children 'helps them to become better human beings' (1974:3); while for Pullman it 'feeds the heart and nourishes the soul and enlarges the spirit' (2004).

Oddly this places children's theatre closer to adult theatre, closer to all theatre and art and means as a result that aesthetic quality becomes of more immediate concern.

The evidence suggests that schools and headteachers are currently aware of this potential, utilising outside experts and companies in theatre more than any other art form. Evidence also suggests that school teachers also feel poorly equipped to deal with theatre on its own terms – lacking art form education and confidence in dealing directly with theatre as art. It is this that needs to be tackled.

Philip Pullman
Theatre – the true key stage

Children need to go to the theatre as much as they need to run about in the fresh air. They need to hear real music played by real musicians on real instruments as much as they need food and drink. They need to read and listen to proper stories as much as they need to be loved and cared for.

The difficulty with persuading grown-up people about this is that if you deprive children of shelter and kindness and food and drink and exercise, they die visibly; whereas if you deprive them of art and music and story and theatre, they perish on the inside, and it doesn't show.

So the grown-ups who should be responsible for providing these good and necessary things – teachers, politicians, parents – don't always notice until it's too late; or they pretend that art and theatre and so on are not necessities at all, but expensive luxuries that only snobbish people want in any case.

The experience of being in the audience when a play is being performed is not simply passive. It's not like watching TV; it's not even like going to the cinema. Everyone in that big space is alive, and everyone is focused on one central activity. And everyone contributes. The actors and singers and musicians contribute their performance; the audience contribute their attention, their silence, their laughter, their applause, their respect.

And they contribute their imagination, too. The theatre can't do what cinema does, and make everything seem to happen literally. So it has limitations. That isn't a real room, it's painted canvas, and it looks like it; that isn't a real boy, it's a little wooden puppet. But the limitations leave room for the audience to fill in the gaps. We pretend these things are real, so the story can happen. The very limitations of theatre allow the audience to share in the acting. In fact, they require the audience to pretend. It won't work if they don't.

The result of this imaginative joining-in is that the story becomes much more real, in a strange way. It belongs to everyone, instead of only to the performers under the lights. The audience in the dark are makers, too. And when it all works, the experience we take away is incomparably richer and fuller and more magical than it would ever have been if all we did was sit back passively and watch.

First published in *The Guardian*, 2004.
Reproduced by permission A P Watt Ltd on behalf of Philip Pullman.

2

From Audience Development
to Cultural Rights

Whether adults choose to watch theatre or not is the result of many significant, if largely invisible, impulses and pressures. These might include whether their own parents went to the theatre; whether they were taken to the theatre as children; whether they took part in drama clubs; the extent of their arts education; where they live and the geographic accessibility of theatre. Whether adults go to the theatre or do not is significantly determined by the experiences, education and inheritances that make up their cultural 'habitus' – more on which later in this chapter. However, whether or not adults go to the theatre is largely a kind of choice.

Children's choices about watching theatre are, in contrast, immediately and explicitly controlled by forces outside themselves. The power balance within our culture that exists between adults and children means that theatre for children is a product made *for* children but is made and consumed in a manner that is far from equal or democratic. As Jonathan Levy notes 'children in the theatre are a captive audience. They do not choose to come. They are brought' (cited in Schonmann, 2006:60-1). Children are a benevolently coerced audience, brought to the theatre by schools, parents or other guardians. They are taken to the theatre perhaps in the same way that children are sent to school or taken to the dentist – because it is good for them.

In thinking about theatre for children it is therefore necessary to think about the relationship between adults and children and the role that theatre occupies within this relationship. Theatre for children is dependent on an often unspoken but usually absolute division of power between adults and children; between author and addressee. In this it is far from unique; this relationship is repeated in other art forms that position themselves as *for* children. In literature, for example, this power imbalance leads Jacqueline Rose to write about the 'impossibility of children's fiction':

> Children's fiction is impossible, not in the sense that it cannot be written (that would be nonsense), but in that it hangs on an impossibility, one which it rarely ventures to speak. This is the impossible relation between adult and child. [...] Children's fiction sets up a world in which the adult comes first (author, maker, giver) and the child comes after (reader, product, receiver). (1984:1-2)

This description could relate equally to theatre for children, where the adult comes first as author, maker, performer, programmer and the child comes after – as audience. The question Rose asks is what 'adults, through literature, want or demand of the child' (1984:137) and similarly with theatre for children the questions we should ask ourselves relate not just to what children want but also to what adults desire for and of children. These are perceptions echoed by Stephen Klein, who writes that

> What might be taken as children's culture has always been primarily a matter of culture produced for and urged upon children [...] Childhood is a condition defined by powerlessness and dependence upon the adult community's directives and guidance. Culture is, after all, as the repository of social learning and socialization; the means by which societies preserve and strengthen their position in the world. (1998:95)

In some ways this is not, again, fundamentally different from the relationship between adults and culture, where cultural consumption can similarly be seen to be governed by forms of social learning and (self-)socialisation. Moreover, while Klein is right that powerlessness is a defining feature of childhood, I would question whether this powerlessness is absolute when it comes to how children engage with, manipulate and use their cultural experiences.

What certainly is the case, however, is that theatre for children is never allowed to be simply for the sake of being. Instead it is always invested with various other qualities, purposes and utilitarian functions whereby the experiencing of theatre will somehow do good to the children concerned. In other words, the status of theatre for children is far from straightforward or comfortable. It is this status that this chapter will largely explore.

Teenaged experiences of theatre

Every year thousands of children are taken on organised visits to the theatre or watch performances by touring companies in their school hall. This is a year-on-year reoccurring cultural activity that is often taken for granted, perhaps seen as assumed knowledge or something that simply happens. For many people their first experiences of theatre are through or at school, and the 'school theatre trip' or performance in the school hall is a familiar cultural phenomenon, known to us from our own memories of childhood.

There are two distinctly separate kinds of activity. The presentation of tailor made productions to young audiences, typically aged under 12, forms the central interest of this book. The other, perhaps more common, is the secondary school trip to the theatre to see main stage productions not specifically aimed at young people. This chapter explores such theatre trips, drawing on research I conducted in 2005 with teenaged audiences from five schools who attended a performance of *Othello* at the Royal Lyceum Theatre, Edinburgh (for a full discussion see Reason, 2006a and 2006b).

It is enlightening to look at how some of the findings of the research were reported in a newspaper article in the Scottish press, and at the letters this generated. The aim is to widen out discussion from the specific piece of research and its participants to more general questions of arts education and cultural policy, and to do so in a manner that highlights the strong social and cultural investment and preconceptions that are at stake: to consider what adults desire of children and young people in their theatrical encounters.

The article, which was in *The Herald*, Scotland's largest circulation quality newspaper, was headlined 'Is it curtains for school theatre trips?' and began:

> The play's the thing? Maybe for *Hamlet*, but not for Scottish pupils attending the theatre, according to new research. Many schoolchildren who attend the theatre give barely a fifth of their attention to what goes on onstage and are instead obsessed with the grandeur of their surroundings, the behaviour of their fellow theatre-goers and their own sense of unease at an unfamiliar experience.
>
> [The research] discovered that in some cases taking pupils to a setting such as the Lyceum appeared to be counterproductive [...] Something that appears very obviously an educational trip is not likely to be an experience pupils will choose to repeat again. (Naysmith, 2005:12)

Although inevitably simplifying and sensationalising the findings, the article was not an outright misinterpretation of the research; the journalist wrote it after reading the published report and interviewing me by telephone. However, the headline and a slightly confrontational tone did unsurprisingly create some ripples in the small world of Scottish theatre and arts education, with several letters published in *The Herald* in response, all reasserting the value of the school theatre trip in both educational and audience development terms and the enjoyment pupils gain from the experience. For example, one letter from a Glasgow teacher stated that 'to assert that theatre trips are an experience which pupils are not likely to 'choose to repeat again' makes my blood boil', while another wrote:

> My colleagues and I were absolutely staggered by the article 'Is it curtains for school theatre trips?' The answer is emphatically NO – and that is from both teachers and pupils here. (*The Herald*, 2005:5)

I am introducing these responses not because the article misrepresented the research, nor because I am wholly unsympathetic to the teachers who responded so passionately. This media debate usefully reminds us of the culturally ingrained position of the school theatre trip within arts education and the level of institutional investment that is placed on the activity. This can be summed up by the perception that such trips are a 'good thing', although it is worth examining some articulations of this rationale.

The secondary school theatre visit is most immediately justified in terms of its educational value, frequently employed to support the study of a play-text or to enhance appreciation of the workings of the theatre for drama students. This was an argument made by all the teachers from secondary schools involved in the research I carried out, with one typical remark being that 'Theatre brings alive a text in a way that television cannot and, for those who find reading inaccessible, a visit to the theatre can help bring a good deal of sense to something that may otherwise have remained a distant 'blur" (personal interview, 2005). Other teachers asserted that the quality of the work produced by pupils was much enhanced following school theatre visits. More broadly, teachers and educators articulate the desire to develop pupils' 'critical faculties' and help make them more discerning or sophisticated audience members (similar comments from teachers are reported in Harland *et al*, 2000:40-2; Downing *et al*, 2003:16-7).

Theatre trips by secondary schools are also articulated as fulfilling broader educational objectives, such as promoting creativity, providing pupils with an understanding of their cultural heritage or encouraging life-long learning after school. In Scotland, the school visit to the theatre, along with other cultural activities, is often presented as supporting 'Learning for Life' through helping 'to equip pupils with the foundation skills, attitudes and expectations necessary to prosper in a changing society and to encourage creativity and ambition'. Again, remarks from teachers affirm this position, one stating that

> I am not just a teacher of English but a teacher of children and I know that a visit to the theatre can be something that pupils will remember for the rest of their lives, it's a real privilege to be able to experience that sense of joy and wonder that kids get. (personal interview, 2005)

Comments such as this also indicate the vocational dedication and personal investment that many teachers have towards organising school theatre visits and other arts activities.

At the same time it is apparent that the theatre to which schools take their pupils is typically of explicit cultural value – or, as the teenage participants in my research put it, 'big dramatic plays' that are 'demanding' and require 'concentration'. This frequently entails seeing works of national significance within the cultural canon, as, in this instance, Shakespeare. This perspective is present in another letter written to *The Herald*, where a teacher stresses her role in introducing pupils to 'serious' or 'difficult' works from the 'cultural canon' and observes that 'If only those children whose parents take them to the theatre have access to centuries' worth of drama then it WILL be an elitist art form. Ignorance will breed ignorance' (*The Herald*, 2005:5).

A similar sentiment is present in observations by Richard Eyre, artistic director of the National Theatre for ten years, who suggested in *The Observer* newspaper in 2007 that schools were failing in precisely this duty to instil in schoolchildren an appreciation of theatre, art and classical music:

> My fears are that [without arts education] you enlarge the divisions in society between those for whom the arts are a part of life and people who think it is impossibly obscure and incomprehensible... I would use the word apartheid. [...] Part of the job of education must be to enfranchise those people who feel disbarred from the arts. I would like to see a co-ordinated strategy between schools and the arts so there is a sense of growing an audience: the consumers of art in the future. (Asthana and Thorpe, 2007)

There are two issues to draw out from this, one of which is contained in the familiar motif of nurturing the audiences of the future; the other is to do with ideas of arts education and what Pierre Bourdieu terms habitus.

Audience development

Eyre's evocation of the audiences of art in the future is a familiar one within the theatre industry. In a relationship often presented as commonsense, theatres are hopeful that in engaging young audiences today they are also engaging their adult audiences of the future. For example, the introduction to the first ever omnibus survey of arts participation amongst secondary school children states that 'It goes without saying that young people form the pool of audiences, participants and arts practitioners of the future' (O'Brien, 1996:1). The Scottish Arts Council argues that 'involvement from an early age is key to an enjoyment, appreciation and engagement that last life-long.' (2006). In general terms, this is the position echoed across the industry; something that John Tulloch identified at the Royal Shakespeare Company, who he describes as being 'as focussed as many banks are in getting their future subscribers early. By these means [...] school students can be encouraged to 'return as adults' to the RSC' (2000:88).

This hope that pupils will return as adults is, of course, shared by the education system. Headteachers, when asked about the role of the arts in primary schools, reveal the perception that 'the benefits of arts education were in part to be drawn upon in later life, when aesthetic appreciation and pleasure in the arts would be a continuing source of enjoyment' (Downing *et al*, 2003:15). Often these beliefs are drawn from teachers' own formative experiences of theatre; one letter writer comments that 'my own love of the theatre was stimulated by a school theatre-goers' group' (*The Herald*, 2005:5).

This relationship between marketing, education and audience development is subject to fierce resistance from some who see the link as incidental, not consequential, and certainly not central to the purpose of arts education work. However, it is also a relationship that is central to a lot of activity that is carried out, particularly by larger-scale arts companies and venues whose primary remit is the production of cultural works and who face the imperative of attracting and retaining audiences. As a result, it is a connection that is repeatedly made in reports and audits seeking to develop the overlaps between marketing and education activities. Indeed, in commissioning an *Education and Audience Development Audit*, the Scottish Arts Council gave the specific remit that it was interested in finding case studies of good practice 'which demonstrate successful links between education and audience development, in that they lead directly to attendance and visits' (Morag Ballantyne, 2001:4). Such approaches are often implicitly motivated by what one piece of research describes as the 'unanimous concern' for 'the theatre to go on living' (Downing *et al*, 2002:26).

Education work does not exclusively take place in terms of young audiences, nor within the formal education system, nor with such direct connection to developing arts attendance. However, as this brief summary suggests, there are extremely deep-rooted understandings motivating school theatre trips –

and the development of young audiences more generally – with institutional investment from both the education and cultural industries, along with significant personal and emotional investment from the teachers and other individuals concerned.

Two implications of this discussion are worth noting. Firstly, while marketing practices at their worst can be seen to seek to infect people with the theatre-going bug through simple *exposure* – that is, putting art in front of people and hoping for the best – much education work specifically tries to go beyond this, enriching and underpinning the experience through workshops, lectures, participation or other activities. In the formal education context, many teachers similarly seek to extend the arts experience through follow up activities and discussions. Such approaches can be understood in terms of facilitating access to the arts through investing knowledge and developing skills, although the danger exists that teenagers fail to appropriate and inter-nalise this knowledge for themselves. The question therefore remains as to how young people develop the theatrical knowledge and skills that are being encouraged when they are exposed to theatre performances, and what impact this has on their ongoing engagement with theatre and other cultural activities.

Secondly, while it is very much hoped that young people enjoy themselves in the moment, this is often accompanied by a sense that, aside from the educational benefit, teenage audiences are not necessarily to be valued for their experiences and responses in and of themselves. Rather they are to be valued for the audiences that they (might) grow into and the critical faculties that they will develop as adults.

The perception is that early arts experience, specifically here of theatre, is crucial to an individual's long term enjoyment of the arts and theatre. While in many ways an unproblematic agenda, the slightly invidious possibility arises that such endeavours are only successful if the children *do* continue to attend as adults, which would negate the value of the experiences in their own right.

Arts habitus

In thinking about this, it is worth introducing Pierre Bourdieu's concept of 'habitus', which broadly refers to the inclinations we have about whether to do one thing or another. Habitus describes our general predisposition to like and seek exposure to certain kinds of things and suggests that what we do and what we consume – whether we choose to go to the theatre, for example – is not random or even necessarily wholly self-aware but instead deeply ingrained into our predispositions and inclinations. The hope with children and young people is that early arts experiences will produce a habitus of theatre-going that they will continue throughout their adult lives.

In terms of the arts, Bourdieu identified two primary factors in determining our cultural habitus – one being arts education, which provides us with greater or lesser 'cultural capital' and thereby the ability to understand and appreciate the art we see; the other being family inheritance. In terms of the relative significance of these two factors, existing research points in both directions.

In 1995 the NFER published a report into the involvement and attendance of young people in the arts. As part of this they explored what factors influenced the disposition, which Bourdieu would term habitus, of young people that determined whether they participated in the arts or not. The primary influences reported were people: significant others in the form of family, particularly mothers, friends and teachers. These were described as 'contagious' influences and were contrasted in the report to the far fewer number of occasions that art experiences themselves were mentioned. Indeed, the report notes that actual theatre experiences were mentioned by young people as a significant element in their being 'turned on' to the arts by only 5 per cent of respondents (Harland *et al*, 1995:184). That actual art experiences are so rarely mentioned as a motivating, or indeed demotivating, factor in engagement with the arts is striking and will be returned to later.

The report explored its findings in terms of social class, and noted amongst its conclusions that 'there seems considerable evidence to suggest that there is a prevalence of parental arts osmosis among the professional classes.' The parallel finding amongst young people from semi-skilled or unskilled backgrounds was that family and friends were much less frequently mentioned as a factor influencing their involvement in the arts – indeed children from this background had much greater difficulty identifying anything that engaged them with the arts. Their conclusion here was that 'the social norms of this category of social class are less likely to include a focus on arts involvement' (Harland *et al*, 1995:182-94). Other research from both the UK and United States affirms this perspective that levels of child arts participation and attendance tend to match that of their parents, suggesting that such inherited 'cultural capital' is crucial (National Endowment for the Arts, 1992; O'Brien, 1996; Harland *et al*, 2000).

In the work I conducted with pupils attending *Othello*, five different schools were involved. One was a private girls' school whose pupils unsurprisingly had a strong sense of entitlement and ownership of the culture on offer, produced by a very direct form of family inheritance. As their teacher remarked, 'I am lucky in that the pupils are generally from backgrounds where middle class parents welcome the idea of their children experiencing theatre and the arts' (personal interview, 2005). Another group of pupils came from a state secondary located in a relatively deprived area but where they were studying drama as a subject in its own right. The rest of the young people were attending with their English Literature teachers. It was noticeable that the pupils studying drama had internalised some of the skills, knowledge and perspective of theatre that allowed them to both possess and critically interrogate their own cultural experiences outside other societal or educational boundaries.

In contrast to such embedded engagement with the arts exhibited in these particular instances, pupils from the other three schools involved believed that theatre simply was not for them. This was articulated in terms of feeling unwelcome, feeling uncomfortable or feeling out of place. As one pupil said, 'you felt like you were in a place where you couldnae speak'; others felt the theatre was a place where they could not be themselves. As various teachers' comments indicate some 'pupils already sense an attitude that suggests that they are not 'worthy' of the theatre' (*The Herald*, 2005:5) or 'there can be a perception that theatre is only for 'snobs'' (personal interview, 2005). In these terms, the rejection of the experience by some of the young people can be seen as a reflection of their lack of a sense of entitlement: a lack of a sense of ownership of both the theatre as a physical entity, of theatre-going as an activity and of the specific cultural product in question. The accessibility of the theatre, therefore, was something that was actively being negotiated by these young audience members through a process that can become a form of self-socialisation, affirming and accepting expected class and cultural boundaries.

This perception that the theatre, or other traditionally high cultural forms, is not 'for them' is a frequent comment found in research into patterns of cultural consumption, particularly amongst young audiences. Scottish Arts Council research, for example, suggests that the feeling of being 'out of place' in an art gallery, museum or theatre, or that such culture is 'not for me', is the experience of 18 per cent of the general population. This increases to 29 per cent for people aged between 16 and 24 (NFO System Three, 2002:50). Harland also suggests in his research that such perceptions are a strong factor in determining that in secondary schools 'the rhetoric of the 'arts as accessible to all' [is] not always borne out in reality' (Harland *et al*, 2000:567). Meanwhile, for many teachers and theatre education workers, overcoming such implicit exclusion and the assertion of entitlement (or, as it was often put more colloquially by the teachers, overcoming perceptions of 'poshness') is the driving motivation for taking young people to the theatre, which becomes an act of asserting their right to be there, their right to ownership of the theatre and of the culture being presented.

Cultural rights

In the UK this moral assertion of the right to be there is prominent within our national discourses about art and culture. It is the right to culture that has resulted in free admission to our national galleries and maintained the drive to keep ticket prices at theatres and other venues low for young people. The concept of a right to culture has also resulted in direct attempts to apply international covenants of cultural rights, more typically employed to defend minority rights in developing countries, to the developed world context of audience development and cultural services provision. Philip Pullman, for example, uses this language very explicitly, writing that children need to go to art galleries, museums and theatre 'so much that human rights legislation alone should ensure that they get them' (2004). In Scotland, a Cultural Commission was established in 2004 with the explicit remit to 'explore the notion of cultural rights for the Scottish Citizen'. Working from the basic premise that 'each citizen of Scotland should have equity of access to cultural activity', the commission sought to define 'a series of cultural rights and consequent cultural entitlements' and identify possible structural and legislative mechanisms for their delivery (Cultural Commission, 2005:30).

It is telling that the words quickly become muddled, shifting from 'rights' and 'entitlements' to 'access', a term much more familiar to arts audience development. The framing of this debate in terms of rights could also be challenged from a variety of perspectives, particularly for the difficulty that arises once any government becomes involved in enshrining basic rights in cultural provision, and the necessity in even the most liberal interpretation to make decisions about what is included and excluded from any definition of culture (for a discussion of this see Donders, 2004; Laaksonen, 2005). As Rodolfo Stavenhagen writes, the right to take part in cultural life enshrined in international law can seem to position culture as a kind of accumulated cultural capital of a nation, which 'some people are able to enjoy [but] others may not have access to' (1998:4). This reasserts the implicitly educational imperative to assist and widen the consumption of what is deemed our national cultural heritage.

The challenge is to construct a discourse that allows us to question some of the assumptions manifested in the school theatre trip, and arts education more generally, without rejecting outright the ideals, convictions and commitment behind them. The belief that everybody has a right to access the institutions, buildings and art forms of their own culture and heritage is something that I firmly believe in. These cultural forms and activities are things that I participate in and value in terms of my own daily life and which are central to my self-identity. I think it is important to stress that the vast majority of the teenagers who took part in the research I conducted both enjoyed and got a lot out of the experience of attending the theatre. They would, like their teachers, assert their absolute *right* to be there and to experience the culture on offer. That is not the same, however, as actively *wanting* to be there. The challenge then is to ask how cultural policy can begin to address some of the issues and perceptions evidenced by young audience members in response to their cultural and, equally importantly, social experiences of the theatre.

In the context of young people and arts education, the concept of a right to take part in cultural life may have a galvanising function. However, in its current form it exists almost entirely in terms of the provision of cultural services and goods – that is, the delivery, promotion and consumption of good cultural products as a good thing. Within this context, the concept of cultural rights bears more than a trace of coercion and relies heavily on the metaphor of infection – exposing young people to the arts in the hope that they catch something. Similarly, for many teachers and educators, the ambition of the school theatre trip and other facilitated cultural activities is to provide young people with as wide a range of experiences as possible and thereby put them in the position of being able to choose for themselves whether or not an art form is for them. The various groups of young people who saw *Othello*, however, were plainly not equally able to make this choice. The assertion of the right to take part in cultural life, in other words, is not the same as overcoming the feeling of being unwelcome or culturally excluded that comes from enduring social, educational and cultural divisions within a society.

Recommendations as to where to go from here are inevitably more difficult than challenging the *ad hoc* nature of much of the current activity and argument. What is apparent from research in this area is that three factors reoccur as significant in a young person's ongoing engagement with the arts, namely: the embedding or internalising of specialist arts education, also known as cultural capital, such as the expert knowledge possessed by drama students in the *Othello* research; family background and the contagious effect of significant others; and, between and across both of these, the internalisation of arts-going into an individual's habitus. What is strikingly absent from this list is art itself. Earlier in this chapter I wrote that only five per cent of young people mention attending a theatre performance as a factor in engaging them with the arts (Harland *et al*, 2000:184). Statistical research in Canada from the 1980s has suggested that 'the experience of being taken to the arts as a child does not significantly affect future attendance' (Morrison and West, 1986:22). Both these pieces of research are open to a variety of criticisms. However, such findings do suggest that the professional arts are largely failing to inspire young people.

There are many reasons for this. It is clear that these do *not* include the question of the right to culture in terms of the unmediated *exposure* of young people to the arts. Here I would agree with Andy Arnold, director of the Arches arts venue in Glasgow, when he states that most people *do* already have access to culture as participants and spectators 'and in its most immediate sense, they have cultural rights'. The problem, he continues:

> is that most people choose not to exercise that right and the challenge is surely to develop an environment where people are stimulated to engage and where the arts are seen as relevant to most people's lives. Few people will attend an opera, Shakespeare play or experimental jazz concert without beforehand becoming conscious to some degree of the worth of these cultural activities. (Arnold, 2005)

In the context of young audiences, the relevance of the arts to their daily lives, outside the education system, is particularly crucial. It should be understood, however, not only in terms of content but also in terms of the form of the cultural product and the nature of the spectator experience. Indeed, it is striking how, in contrast to the provision made for adult audiences and younger children, little theatre or art is produced specifically for the teenage audience (Young Scot, 2004:34). Tony Graham also observes this deficiency, writing that 'apart from the Contact Theatre in Manchester, there are precious few building spaces where work aimed at teenagers is welcome. The idea that work should stop being presented at twelve strikes me as very strange' (2005: 84). The reasons for this situation might in part be because of the difficulty of doing so without coming across as patronising or ghettoising. However, it is also because the objective for the cultural experience, or tellingly cultural education, with such groups is often projective and in preparation for their future enjoyment as adults, rather than in terms of their immediate enjoyment as audiences in their own right. Crucially, to suggest that arts events might be more directly tailored for a teenage audience is not to question the competence, attention span or intelligence of the audience, but instead to recognise the specificity of their lived experience.

What is important is that cultural rights do not relate solely to physical or economic access or simply exposure – which might be crudely characterised as the practical matter of getting young children through the door – but also encompass the social, cultural and knowledge barriers that inhibit engagement with the arts. These barriers frequently take the form of questions of competency and of knowledge (or cultural capital). Without the required knowledge and abilities, children and young people will be largely unable to access a production. Or alternatively, they may grasp certain aspects but will be uncomfortable or unable to take the experience onto other levels. The right to culture, therefore, also depends on the fulfilment of a right to knowledge and personal empowerment.

Connected to this, it is vital to recognise the significance of pupils' own perceptions and attitudes to the effectiveness of any arts education, whatever the final ambitions might be. Theatre-going is a learned activity, governed by a complex set of cultural values and implied social codes, which individuals need to adopt for themselves if they are to internalise a sense of entitlement, ownership and legitimacy as members of the audience. The hope has always been that early and teenage experiences of theatre have the potential to embed or at least normalise the activity of theatre-going.

The evidence of research into teenage audiences, including that briefly presented in this chapter, indicates that too often young people are merely exposed to theatre with little sense of a personal investment in or ownership of the culture in question. Instead of being relevant to their lives, or perceived as being theirs, the experience is very much of culture as other – both in terms of content and of form – and in this sense it is worth little to them in their daily or imaginative lives.

In my research there were two distinct exceptions to this. Firstly, those from the girls' private school and with the most privileged background, who had internalised and inherited a sense of entitlement to the arts. Secondly, from the group of pupils who were studying drama as a subject in its own right, who had internalised the skills, knowledge and perspectives that allowed them to both possess and value their own cultural experiences and take them outside either societal or educational boundaries. Tellingly, theatre and other arts subjects are often marginalised in schools' academic curricula, an act that in itself helps perpetuate a perceived lack of value or relevancy (Harland *et al*, 2000:568).

The right to culture seems unquestionable. However, it needs to be released from being employed as a concept to aid the delivery of other educational or social goods or being seen in terms of the exposure metaphor and questions of audience development. Indeed, in this context any formalised cultural rights are of questionable validity as, in order to be fully achieved and realised, all rights need to be internalised. Delivered from outside, the right to culture is an abstract construct, at best something exotically enjoyable but fundamentally other. Internalised, participation in cultural life becomes fundamental to an individual's self-identity and truly inalienable. Informal cultural rights, therefore, would be about providing young people with the skills in spectatorship, the confidence and the knowledge that allows them to take possession of the cultural forms on offer on their own terms and in their own right. To develop these critical abilities, age-appropriate cultural ex- periences need to be embedded throughout the education system from primary school onwards.

One particularly powerful concern is that too much focus on the audience developmental potential of taking children and young people to the theatre ignores, or at least undervalues, their importance as an audience in their own right. To perceive young people's engagement with theatre as primarily about audience development is to value the adult audience they *might* become, rather than the audience they are now.

This importance of ensuring that productions are suitable and rewarding for their audiences at that particular moment in their lives, is something evoca- tively asserted in Martin Drury's description of the importance of presentness:

> Children are not the audience of the future. Rather, they are citizens of the here-and-now, with important cultural entitlements. An 8 year old is not a third of a 24 year old, a quarter of a 32 year old, or a fifth of a 40 year old. Being 8 is a whole experience ... there are understandings and meanings particular to being 8. (2006:151)

It is here that the value and strength of theatre produced specifically for children and young people lies. So it is vital that we pay attention to what that particular experience of being eight years old means in relation to children's responses to live theatre.

Tony Graham
Children grow up not down

The idea of 'theatre for children' has always struck me as strange. It may once have served a purpose. Like any emerging social movement, separatism is a healthy stage but it can lead to narrowness and a ghetto mentality. Theatre for children suggests a tight seal around the audience and a restricted age range. It encourages all manner of nonsense: didacticism, moralising (what Carl Miller calls 'theatre of ought'), low standards (theatre of nought?), the cheap, the cheerful, the simplistic, the infantile. Such ideas have nothing to do with children and everything to do with well-meaning adults.

Why then at the Unicorn in London have we built a new theatre whose declared purpose is to create and present the best work for children and young audiences? The most salient reason is to nurture a kind of theatre that includes a child's perspective. Coined in the 1960s, 'a child's perspective' remains a revolutionary idea. It challenges those who write and create but, equally, has implications for every facet of theatre for the young. If we are to create great theatre which contains this perspective, it is essential to build that house. Under what circumstances can the best theatre for young audiences flourish? Do we have the necessary time, space and resources to research, witness and create such work?

Do the young feel welcome? Can they see and feel the show? Do we even care what they think? And how are we to find out? Is it a rich experience for them? Are we able to extend theatre into a more active form of engagement and participation? How do children experience theatre when people of different ages are present? Whatever else they might imply, these are also architectural questions. They influence the arrangement of space and how we all move through it.

But none of this matters one tiny bit if the work doesn't connect with audiences. At our theatre we have devised a five-pronged chart for writers and makers which helps us to gauge scripts. The five prongs (think of a star as they are all connected) are: poetry, substance, transcendence, dramatic potential and a child's perspective. These criteria help us to assess if something has earned its place at our theatre. Whether it's written or devised, adapted or original; whether it begins with a script or has another starting-point are secondary matters. The main thing is quality; the electricity of a palpable hit. The point at which a theatre experience grabs hold of us in a way that penetrates our emotional shield and lifts us out of our seats. And leads to some infinitesimal change. Otherwise, why bother?

But the paradox remains. It can take an infinite number of forms but theatre for young audiences, if it's to be any good, must by definition be theatre for all of us. We live in the same world as children. It's no less complex and baffling for children than it is for the rest of us. We're lying if we say we know the answers. So 'theatre for children' should be banned by the Trades Description Act. At best it's partial, at worst it's misleading. To be good enough for children, it has to be good enough for the rest of us. And if you or I don't really care about it, why on earth should they? But, and here's the thing, it's not possible to make theatre for all of us unless we respect childhood, growing up, and adolescence.

A radical shift in perception about theatre for young audiences will surely happen in this century. It has already started, but we're on a long journey. And along the way, we'll need to change how we see and describe ourselves. In putting an end to theatre for children, we might be able to create a theatre of which children and all of us could be proud.

Tony Graham is Artistic Director of the Unicorn Theatre, London

3

Quality in Theatre for Children

As an art form, theatre for children often goes out of its way to assert its seriousness, importance and standards of excellence. The Scottish Arts Council, for example, states that today 'Scotland's theatre companies strive – and succeed – in offering the same high standards of quality in children's theatre as those in mainstream theatre' (2006). The same sentiments would be true across the UK and abroad, where the quality and status of theatre for children *as theatre* are prominently supported.

While the reputation of theatre for children has risen over the last decade, this idea of quality and its validity as an art form in its own right is not necessarily indicative of widespread perceptions. For a long time theatre for children has had a mixed reputation. One reason is that it often straddles the worlds of subsidised, commercial and community theatre, often serving competing purposes of entertainment and education, often slipping between competing criteria of quality and utility.

In 2002 the Arts Council of England (ACE) organised a seminar on 'the quality of children's theatre'. Amongst the many testimonies collected as to the importance of theatre for children were many assertions of a lack of 'quality', respect and investment. For example, Anthony Clark, director of the Hampstead Theatre in London, argued that 'children's theatre seems to lack kudos in the profession and the theatre itself lacks kudos with children' (2002:26). Similarly, journalist and critic Lyn Gardner stated that 'theatre for young people is underfunded, critically ignored and denied a central place in the culture' (2002:32).

Evidence from the ACE seminar report and other sources would also suggest that within the United Kingdom it continues to be the case that, outside seasonal productions, particularly panto, children's and family performances are largely excluded from the main subsidised, building-based producing companies. There are, of course, notable exceptions to this, including the work of the National Theatres of both Scotland and England. For example, amongst the first productions of the then new National Theatre for Scotland in 2007 was *Wolves in the Walls*, aimed at the whole family and demonstrating a commitment to producing work for young audiences, while the National Theatre in London produced Philip Pullman's *His Dark Materials* in 2003. Nonetheless, there remains the perception that theatre for children is 'an add-on' rather than something integrated with the rest of a company's work (Clark, 2002:27). Reasons for this are numerous, including that family productions and theatre for children tend to generate less income, because ticket prices are necessarily lower to ensure access. This puts pressure on the productions to cost less, re-enforcing perceptions of lack of worth and lack of quality.

The somewhat marginalised position of theatre for children within theatre as a whole is maintained for other reasons as well. Due to vastly lower costs for both schools and theatre companies, most primary school children see theatre performances in their school rather than in a theatre. There are many financial and practical advantages to this, including the possibility of increasing access, not least in rural areas. However, there is also widespread concern within the industry about what such productions imply about the nature of the art form. Clark, for example, argues that it

> has the effect, unfortunately, of marginalising the work within the profession, and limiting a child's experience of the full potential of this collaborative medium. Most damaging of all perhaps, is the fact that the theatre becomes synonymous with the small scale, school and education (2002:28)

Leading on from this, there has at times been a dismissive attitude within the wider theatre industry towards productions for children, viewed as 'schools theatre', as settling for lower standards and perceived as 'a poor, second-division area of theatre in which to cut one's teeth or mark time' (Wood, 2005: 114). Indeed, Reekie suggests that prior to the early 1990s most theatre for children in Scotland was 'horribly poor':

> The work was cheap, under-produced, under-rehearsed, variations on pantomime with enough audience participation to keep the audiences from catching breath to realise what rubbish it all was. (2005:38)

Finally there is a deep-rooted, much questioned but continuing presumption that theatre for children is somehow second best. Something that actors or directors might do while waiting for something better to come along, but rarely out of choice.

What is quality?

Quality in theatre for children might be considered wholly or largely subjective, a matter of taste or fashion. Quality might also be applied, not insignificantly, to the physical and material standards of a production. Quality might alternatively, but more problematically, be related to the effectiveness of theatre for children at delivering various instrumental benefits, as discussed in previous chapters, whether to individual children, to schools or to communities as a whole. Quality might, therefore, be related to some universalised and timeless judgement of taste or reduced to the specific needs and requirements of a particular audience at a particular time.

Whatever concept or standard is adopted, one common assertion is that theatre for children should be 'of quality' – whatever that is – in the same way that any theatre should be of quality. Writing in 1974, for example, Moses Goldberg declares:

> 'High standards' in the children's theatre means basically the same thing as does 'high standards' in the adult theatre: artistically unified productions that achieve the highest possible quality in each area of theatrical endeavour. (1974:23)

A little later Goldberg quotes Stanislavski as saying 'it is necessary to act for children as well as for adults, only better' by way of declaring that 'the principles of acting and the need for good acting are identical in adult and children's theatre' (1974:23).

As Shifra Schonmann explores in her book, *Theatre as a Medium for Children and Young People*, this idea that children's theatre is basically the same as adult theatre was particularly prominent in the 1970s. At its heart is the desire for the art form not to be treated as substandard and not to be defined as deficient in any manner. However, while the idea of equality might be important, the suggestion of sameness is more problematic. Schonmann, for example, quotes Korogodsky (1978) as suggesting that

> The only factor that distinguishes youth theatre from the stage for grownups is the fact that the spectators are children. (cited in Schonmann, 2006:16)

This one difference should also be seen as the most fundamental difference of all, a perspective that Schonmann asserts passionately, suggesting that:

> I see this view as one of the most important causes that prevent the theatre for young audiences from developing its own theatrical genres. [It has] narcotized the imagination of actors and directors and their curiosity to search for new forms of artistic performance suitable for the youngest audiences. (2006:17)

The difference in the audience, in other words, is the most fundamental and important difference of all, because the measure of quality needs to be set against the particular forms and manner of perception suitable for a young audience. As Phyllis Lutley writes:

> It is theatre – not simplified Adult Theatre, children are not simplified adults – but theatre of the kind which we have come to believe is right for young children. (Lutley and Demmery, 1978:1)

Here the assertion of quality is present – it is theatre, not something lesser or different – but also the declaration that it should be made for children as they are and not adjusted or, worse, simplified, from existing models or methods.

The fear is, of course, that if the standards of theatre for children are agreed to be different then – because of pressures on funding and the history of the form – almost inevitably the standards will also be lower. With this in mind, the quality of much theatre for children has been questioned. Gardner, for example, sees a mawkish, sentimental nostalgia in much work produced for children, both in writing and theatre, observing '[we] wouldn't dare treat adults like that but hell, it's for a family audience so who will notice?' (2002: 34).

What is certainly the case is that productions touring schools can be operating with limited resources, working to a low baseline and required to deliver work across a wide age range. The results are not necessarily unpopular nor unentertaining and one very legitimate response to those who doubt the 'quality' of much theatre for children is that its immediate success and enjoyment by its actual audiences is often not in doubt. If children are enjoying the experience, and surely there is nothing wrong with pure good fun, then what more can be asked and to what extent are complaints motivated by subjective taste or by class and elitism?

It is here that the richness, the fullness, distinctiveness or *potential* of the audience experience of theatre is relevant. It is a question of our perception of the abilities and nature of young people as an audience and of our ambitions for that audience.

Respecting the young audience

Not all theatre made for children is of the highest quality – neither is all theatre for adults. However, while not mistaking children for simplified adults, nor believing that the two forms are or need to be the same, it is worth thinking about quality a bit more in terms of the ambitions that we have for theatre productions, whether for children or adults.

If we think about what we might describe as the worst habits within theatre for children, it is possible to get away with a lot through audience participation, loudness and effectively driving your audience into a state of distracted hyperventilation. Similarly with theatre for adults, and with entertainment more generally, it is possible to get away with a lot and deliver very little if a production is immediately diverting, whether through sex, violence, spectacle or virtuosity. Most adult theatre or entertainment makes very limited demands upon its audience, except to sit back, watch and have a largely passive experience.

While this is a subjective question and a subjective set of perceptions, it is fairly reasonable to state that much entertainment does not explicitly set out to do any more than that, and within such ambitions there is nothing wrong with sheer entertainment. Similarly with theatre for children, there is nothing fundamentally wrong with sheer entertainment if nothing more is claimed or desired. However, saying there is nothing wrong with it, is not to say there are not some limitations, or that more is not possible.

There is a suggestion that theatre for children has, particularly in the past but at times still today, often settled for doing nothing more. It does not say much about our perceptions of the abilities of young children if we settle for baseline productions. It suggests that for young audiences it is not necessary to do more because children either do not need more, would not understand greater subtlety, or would not actively appreciate greater variety. Gardner argues that one of the major reasons for the poor quality of much theatre for children lies 'in our attitudes towards children themselves and the concept and construct of childhood' (2002:33). Children, in other words, are sentimentalised in our society but also silenced and marginalised. A lack of respect for the abilities of child audiences implies that they are not worth more. Caryl Jenner, one of the pioneers of theatre for children at the Unicorn Theatre in London, suggests that we often underrate a child's powers of perception and make cultural products made for them too simple or too one-dimensional. In contrast, Jenner demands that we respect the abilities and ambitions of the child audience (cited in Ford and Wooder, 1997). It is these ambitions, and this respect for the abilities of its audience that we can use as a marker of quality in theatre for children. It is these aspects that enable us to recognise quality amongst the work that is being produced.

Note how Brian McMaster articulates the nature of quality in the arts in his 2008 report 'Supporting Excellence in the Arts'. McMaster consciously embraces the task of attempting a definition of excellence, writing that

> Excellent culture takes and combines complex meanings, gives us new insights and new understandings of the world around us and is relevant to every single one of us. [...] The best definition of excellence I have heard is that excellence in culture occurs when an experience affects and changes an individual. An excellent cultural experience goes to the root of living. (2008:9)

Children are scarcely mentioned in the document; nowhere is it stated that McMaster is explicitly including or excluding art for children and young people in his discussion. His notion of excellence, however, is equally legitimate and useful as a statement in relation to theatre for children. Vitally for me, McMaster links quality to the 'excellence of the experience', meaning it is neither abstract nor technical but about the nature of the audience's engagement. Quality in a cultural experience is its enduring resonance as it engages us intellectually, imaginatively or emotionally. A marker of quality in a work of art is its ability to make us look for longer. This is certainly the case with theatre made for adults and we should have the same ambitions in theatre made for children.

That young children can understand and respond to complex and subtle theatrical performances is something asserted anecdotally by many practitioners who have worked with children. Jain Boon, for example, recalls the experience of post-show discussion with young audience members, writing 'I am always surprised at how able these young children are at articulating and recognising the characters' thoughts and feelings. They are able to pick up on what is unsaid' (2005:175). That children's ability to read and follow a performance is constantly surprising, even to those working in this area, is an indication, perhaps, of the temptation to underestimate the audience that Jenner describes. The perimeters and extent of this theatrical competence is explored in later chapters of this book.

What is at stake with theatre for children, therefore, is in part a question of how we view children and the ambitions we have for them: most immediately as audience members, but also as thinking and creative individuals. Quality in terms of ambition relates not just to what theatre directors believe they can show their audience, but also how much they believe an audience can bring to a production and how far they can travel with it afterwards. This is something that Philip Pullman articulates in the text reproduced in this book when he describes how in any comparison between theatre and television or film, it is the *limitations* of the live performance that are important along with the work done *by the audience* that brings the experience to life.

Quality in theatre for children relates to the medium itself and not, or at least not only, to the explicit content of a production. What is it, in other words, that requires the audience to be there, in that space, at that time? How is this theatre? Meaning, how distinctly theatre and using the full characteristics and possibilities of theatre, and not some other form or media? Moreover, in respecting the young audience, it is surely valuable to consider children's own awareness and understanding of the medium, their own sense of why they are watching theatre, their own reflections upon the medium itself.

Ambition in theatre for children relates to respecting and not patronising the audience. It also relates to making the audience work, making them contribute their imagination to a production and through doing so making them think and feel. This is often a matter of including a greater range of tones, emotions and senses, or not providing all the answers or making things one-dimensional or simple. As Tony Graham, director of the Unicorn Theatre in London writes, 'The enemy is the literal, the safe, the convenient and the tendency to reduce. Our job is not to make simpler' (2005:39).

Ambition in theatre for children is therefore about transforming a passive audience of consumers into an active audience: not necessarily in terms of direct audience participation, but in terms of emotional and intellectual engagement. Engagement, that is, with both the play of theatre and the exploration of life. The result, as Clark writes, is something that is more than simple entertainment, which goes further and lasts longer and means more:

> The harder the child, just like an adult, is working to discover meaning the greater their commitment to the event and the more lasting the effect. Thought, ideas and solutions, emerge from complex, perplexing, uncomfortable situations. Shallow scripts, banal themes, an explicit message, and the absence or irony and ambiguity make for bad theatre. (2002:29)

Similar ideas are expressed by Jeanne Klein, in an articulation of what she believes should be the ambitions of theatre for children, where she describes the need to aim to do more than provide 'escapist entertainment requiring little mental investment.' Instead, she says, children 'should have deeply moving experiences, hold images from these experiences in their memories, and think critically when they attend their next theatrical events' (1993:13).

Theatre as theatre

While at times theatre for children has occupied a second-rate position within the arts, there are those who seriously believe in its value and potential. At its best, theatre for children is amongst the most imaginative, challenging and rewarding forms of theatre around. As playwright John Clifford observes, 'perhaps the really important challenge is to create adult theatre that is as good as, and as profound as, and as profoundly entertaining as, the best children's theatre' (2000:72). From the perspective of those producing work with and for young people, therefore, doing so is a positive choice, one stimulated by the excitement and creativity of wanting to thrill and entertain a particularly demanding and rewarding audience.

This producing and programming of theatre for children on the part of practitioners and companies can be described as a movement or interest within the artistic community that engages in theatre *as theatre*. That is, an artistic community producing theatre as a creative, experience-focused activity, with the primary motivation being the enjoyment and reward of the activity itself. This is the focus of the research presented in the next section of this book, which explores the responses of young children to the experience of watching *theatre as theatre*.

Peter Manscher and Peter Jankovic
Eye-level

In Denmark, over the past 30 or 40 years or so, we have developed a certain approach to making theatre for children and young people that we call 'eye-level theatre'. The following quotation sums up very precisely the double meaning of the general Danish 'eye-level' concept:

> We believe that children are entitled to theatre of the highest quality.
>
> They have the need to share our thoughts, as adults, on life and death.
>
> To be given wholesome stories they understand, and not just slops.
>
> To be entertained, surprised, to laugh and cry in sympathy with the characters they see on stage, right in front of them.
>
> The ambition is to create shows that highlight acting in a simple set.
>
> We play for a limited number of spectators at a time. Every child must feel – both during and after the show – that: '...if I hadn't been there, the show would have been different.'

So the eye-level concept functions both on a philosophical and a physical level.

Danish theatre for children is all about creating a dialogue between the performer and the audience. Not always a concrete dialogue during the performance, but always a dialogue in which artists try to create a philosophical meeting place between the child and the adult – in order to share experiences and to learn something from one another, seeing 'eye-to-eye' on stories and issues of mutual interest.

The physical meeting place is usually not in a theatre at all, but in the children's everyday environment in gym-halls, libraries, classrooms, cultural centres, or kindergartens. So the sets need to be easily transportable, and the technical requirements not exceeding those which are generally available in such places.

On a practical level, it also means that actors seldom play on an elevated stage, but prefer to perform on the floor, directly 'eye-to-eye' with a small number of spectators that we can see and relate to, rather than in front of a large, anonymous audience.

Personally, we are particularly fond of this remark from a 7 year old child on the 5th row after having witnessed a children's theatre performance: 'This is for me. This was exactly what I wanted to see, but I just didn't know until I saw it.' This is probably the best we can do in our work.

Peter Manscher, Secretary General of the 2011 ASSITEJ World Congress (www.assitej 2011.info) and Festival Programmer at Teatercentrum (www.teatercentrum.dk)

Peter Jankovic, Composer and Dramaturg, Theatre Lampe (www.teatret-lampe.dk).

Part Two
The Theatrical Experience

4

Researching Children's Lived Experiences of Theatre

The previous chapters explored how early encounters with theatre and live performance are often described as providing valuable experiences in the broad social, cultural and creative development of children and young people. Early experiences are seen as crucial in terms of long-term enjoyment of theatre. The hope – not always fulfilled – is that such encounters will develop a cultural habitus of theatre going and internalise a sense of ownership of the arts.

The potential for theatre to play a role in delivering a range of educational, social and cultural benefits is reflected in a growing body of research. This research primarily explores the direct or indirect use of theatre as a tool of socio-cultural development: in formal or informal education; in promoting creativity; or in building future audiences. What such research largely ignores is the lived experience of theatre. Actual audiences do not experience theatre in terms of its potential instrumental rewards. Instead, theatre is experienced *as theatre*: something that is responded to in terms of pleasure and emotion; interpretation and evaluation.

There exists little field-based, qualitative research which illuminates what the actual theatre experience means *as theatre* to young audiences, or indeed, of the experiences of theatre audiences as a whole. Talking to audiences is, as Helen Freshwater describes it in *Theatre and Audiences*, the 'road less travelled' in theatre research (2009:27). In an academic context, most discussion of audiences takes the form of largely theoretical perspectives (for example Bennett, 1997). Some work, however, does exist in terms of qualitative exploration of young people's and children's experiences of theatre. For example, John Tulloch (2000) has explored how teenager's theatre experiences are often directed by the school and educational context, with some of the implications of this discussed in Chapter Two. Willmar Sauter's book *The Theatrical Event* (2000) includes a short chapter of research into primary school children's theatrical experiences, which is explored in more detail in Chapter Five. In the United States Jeanne Klein has, over several years, been exploring children's aesthetic responses to theatre (1987, 1989, 1990, 1993 and 2005); while Shifra Schonmann's 2006 publication, *Theatre as a Medium for Children and Young People,* is the only other book-length work in this area. The work of both Schonmann and Klein is explored later in this book.

In contrast to the lack of formal research into the theatrical experiences of children, there are countless and largely uncollected narratives of anecdotal and experience-based knowledge possessed by teachers, parents, theatre practitioners and others who engage with young children as they encounter theatre performances. The material presented in the following chapters sets out to complement this anecdotal knowledge through detailed and carefully structured qualitative audience research. Most of this research was conducted through participative arts-based workshops involving groups of primary school children and the insights provided are explored in depth. First, however, I interrogate the research objectives and methodologies so as to make clear the nature and qualities of the subsequent analysis.

The lived experience

The research and analysis presented in this book focuses on children's lived experiences of theatre, on what they remember, how they construct meanings, the stories they tell and the knowledge they have. When children go to the theatre we might hope or expect that they are entertained, illuminated, educated or inspired. In conversation we might speak of a performance *doing* something for us; or talk about taking something away from a production. In other words, we are interested not just in the production but in our experience of the production. The systematic attempt to uncover such experiences is described in media and cultural studies as ethnographic audience research, defined as empirical research investigating 'cultural practices as lived experience' (Geraghty, 1998:142). Transposing such approaches to theatre, Henri Schoenmakers describes how ethnographic approaches allow us to gain insights into 'the theatrical experiences as considered important by the spectators themselves' (1990:98-100).

In thinking about lived experiences, I followed the perspective of phenomenological philosophy which describes knowledge as rooted in encounter and experience. Phenomenology is 'the study of objects and events as they present to, and appear in, our experience' (Burnard, 2000:8). Within this world-view, far more meaningful and revealing material results from working with participants and their conscious knowledge of their selves and experiences than from treating them as passive vessels or inactive consumers. Experience is actively constructed by the individual: the phenomenology of being in the theatre can only be known through asking each individual to engage with the experience for themselves.

The emphasis of this research, therefore, is not on the educational or social benefits of theatre for children, but on experiential perceptions; focusing on young audience members' experiences in terms of their engagement with the theatrical spectacle, with different levels of illusion and reality, with theatrical technique and convention. The discussion seeks to enhance our understanding of how children remember and respond to theatrical experiences imaginatively, intellectually and emotionally. The insights provided should assist art providers and educators in developing their own knowledge about children's theatrical engagement.

Visual arts workshops

In seeking to uncover what theatrical experiences mean within an audience's enduring memory, one challenge, of course, is exactly how to access and uncover such meanings. Approached cold by a stranger and asked to talk about one's experiences of art or theatre, most people would be a little hesitant, unforthcoming, unengaged, perhaps even suspicious. With children these elements are enhanced, and their likely answers would be short and lacking detail. In seeking to uncover a rich and detailed description of how young children respond to, remember and engage with theatre, it was therefore necessary to adopt a methodology that would be engaging, reassuring and appropriate for their levels of understanding, their interests and their particular skills and abilities. Such appropriateness is important with all research with people, but particularly vital when working with children. The solution was an approach that used visual arts workshops, children's drawings, and conversations about those drawings, as tools through which to engage with children and explore their recent theatre experience.

In using drawing and painting, the methodology drew on established approaches in disciplines that use various visual or creative tools to interact with research participants. This includes what are known as 'projective techniques' within forensic evidence gathering, clinical psychology and market research; creative-reflective techniques within media research (Gauntlett,

2004); and the long established use of drawing within art therapy. These approaches are motivated by the idea that when responding to direct questioning, people may be reluctant or not consciously able to reveal their true attitudes or deepest feelings. To address this difficulty, researchers use methods designed to allow participants to project their feelings or opinions through various stimuli such as word association tests, sentences and story completion, photo sorts and art.

As the participants in my research were primary school children, the use of drawing and visual art seemed to be particularly suitable, being an age appropriate means of expression with which they would be familiar and comfortable. The centrality of drawing to children's sense of themselves and their communicative repertoires is something stressed across a variety of disciplines; drawing is a different kind of activity for children than it is for adults. As Pia Christiansen writes, children themselves consider 'all' children to be competent at drawing, which is an ordinary rather than specialised activity (Christensen and James, 2000:167). This perception is broadly reversed amongst adults. At the same time, drawing ability is of course hugely influenced by children's developmental stage. For this study, therefore, it was vital to be aware of the stages of ability in visual perception and communication through which children progress, particularly in terms of the use of representational schema.

As the workshops were to be focused around drawing activities, and to mark them as different from schoolwork and classroom tasks, it was decided to engage the children immediately with drawing and visual art materials. The workshops began with some warm-up drawing games, such as getting children to 'take a line for a walk' or draw portraits of themselves without taking their pen off the paper. I and the other workshops facilitators joined in these games, using our own drawings to model to the children examples of different drawing styles and abilities and provide an opportunity to explain that we were not concerned with their relative abilities in drawing, but rather with them doing their best. Only rarely did we face objections to the task of drawing, which the children were largely very happy with. For example, in this exchange the children as a group answer a classmate's concern about drawing ability:

> **Marc**: What happens if we're not good at drawing?
>
> **Zoe**: That doesn't really matter.
>
> **Jodi**: You just do your best.

Jack: Yeah!

Robbie: Just take your time.

Following these exercises, the bulk of the workshops consisted of a period of largely unstructured free drawing, which was intended to provide the opportunity for the children to produce pictures drawn from their memory of the theatre performance. We began with a non-limiting opening request, asking the children to 'draw something you remember from the performance'.

Drawing and talk

As the children drew, we moved around the room, talking to individuals as they worked, or as they finished a particular drawing, and asking them to tell us about the performance and about their drawing. Our conversation with the children often began with a deliberately open-ended question along the lines of 'tell me about your drawing'. This was followed by questions or conversation as led by the child, the drawing or the situation. The intention was to use drawings as a way in to extended conversations with children about their experiences.

This connection between children drawing and talking is well established. As Malchiodi describes it, 'drawing naturally relaxes many children who become absorbed in the task and leads them to want to share information' (1998:48). Similarly, according to Angela Anning, for children there exists a close connection between talk and drawing, with children often drawing a picture and telling a story at the same time. In this context both drawing and storytelling talk are tools with which children 'order and explain the complexity of their experiences of the world' (Anning and Ring, 2004:5).

Although theoretically fairly straightforward, it is important not to neglect the subtleties required to achieve these objectives, particularly the nature of our questioning and conversation. Several writers have noted some of the difficulties in talking to children. In her discussion about the relationship between children's talk and their drawings, Elizabeth Coates contrasts the lively, dramatic and spontaneous narratives that children produce when talking to themselves while drawing (particularly younger children aged 3-6) with the more 'stilted and short descriptions' provided if asked to talk about their drawings more formally afterwards (2004:8-10). Rhoda Kellogg notes in the context of art therapy that the uneven power balance between adults and children means that children may accept adults' responses and assessments even though they are not true interpretations (cited in Coates, 2004:7). Sheila Green observes that 'children may give answers that are determined more by the desire to please than their desire to be truthful' (Greene and Hill, 2005:9). Karen Saywitz describes how children can assume that interviewers already know the answers to the questions they are asking and seek to comply with them (2002:10).

The precise nature of the questioning and conversational technique is therefore vital. It is easy to slip into a school mode of 'benevolent but relentless questioning' where 'teacher questions and child responds' (Anning and Ring, 2004:31). I noticed in my own questioning, for instance, that I was slipping into a mode of testing children's memory of the performances and rewarding them with praise when they got a particular detail or recollection correct.

Such testing of memory does not enhance or extend children's post-performance experience – the opposite, in fact, as it marks the performance as something fixed, external and in the past. The ambition should instead be to use open questioning to elicit multi-word responses in which the children can articulate their experience from their own perspective (Malchiodi, 1998: 50-2; Saywitz, 2002:9). Saywitz suggests using 'wh- questions' (who, what, where, why, how) as 'open-ended questions avoid implying that the adult prefers a particular response' (2002:9). I have found, however, that 'why' questions, although instinctive, are generally best avoided. Asking 'why', particularly with a grown-up talking to a child, often implies or becomes a kind of test, as if seeking some kind of explanation. Asking 'why did you draw it like this?' can produce post-event rationalisations that do not reflect the actual processes of creation or thought.

In contrast, I have found there is often particular value in asking a question along the lines of 'how did you know...?' The nature of this question – how did you know it was a sunny day? How did you know the prince was sad? How did you know...? – means that the answers children provide are likely to return to what they saw and drew. Essentially the question asks children to think about the reasons behind their decisions in making their drawings and usefully elicits the skills that children employ when responding to a performance. Crucially, it also reveals these skills, which can be implicit or unconscious, to the children themselves, making them more aware of their own capacities.

Coming from a background in art therapy, Malchiodi suggests a slightly different range of approaches, such as the questioner wondering out loud about elements of the drawing ('I wonder what this person is thinking?') in order to imply a stance of not knowing and giving children the opportunity to explain the drawing from their perspective (1998:50-2).

Figure 4.1: 'Tell me about your drawing'. Research workshops in progress. Facilitator Alison Reeves. Photograph by Brian Hartley.

Open-ended, non-leading questions:
Tell me about your drawing?
What is going on in this picture?
Playful, interpretative, stimulating questions:
How do the people/animals in this picture feel?
If they could speak, what would they say?
What title would you give your drawing?

Thus I sought to use drawing as a tool with which to engage and interact with the participating children. The drawings produced would in themselves provide one kind of evidence of experience, but would also be objects through which to initiate and mediate conversation. This was because while getting the children to produce drawings was an engaging and appropriate way of working with them, it presented potentially huge problems concerning interpretation and analysis. The ambiguity of visual representations, and the diversity of possible explanations for precisely why a drawing looks the way it does, are significant stumbling blocks to the use of non-verbal techniques in any piece of research or participatory practice. Tellingly, when children's drawings are used as evidence in a legal or forensic context where the objective is factual accuracy, it is recognised that 'interpreting what children do (or draw) is considerably more risky than listening to what they say' (Pipe *et al*, 2002:170).

Not knowing

Faced with such problems, the current trend in art therapy with children has been away from the diagnostic use of art, that is the attempt to interpret the content of a visual artefact based upon its appearance alone, and instead towards an approach that explores children's drawings through a child's own verbalisation and discussion about their drawings (Malchiodi, 1998:41-43). In other words, children are asked to talk about their own drawings and, rather than the therapist becoming the expert analyser, the child becomes the primary interpreter of the visual artefacts they create. It is this combination of drawing and talk that forms the methodological key to this research. The drawings themselves are extremely striking, provocative, different, intriguing and immediate, making it tempting to value them over the transcribed conversations. However, neither aspect should be perceived as dominant, either in terms of the analysis of the results or of the process of the workshops themselves. For although I have described the workshops as visual arts based, in fact the process was a combination of drawing and talk, with the children engaging with their experiences through drawing, but also through careful questioning and directed conversation.

In a connected debate, other writers have asserted the importance of recognising the knowledge that children possess, rather than overriding this knowledge with the assertion of superior adult expertise. The ethical importance of doing this should be clear, but this is combined with a methodological and epistemological purpose. As Morrow and Richards put it, if we talk to children about the meanings and emotions that they attach to their drawings then we also engage with the 'talent that they, as children, possess' (1996:100). Similarly, Berry Mayall notes that if the objective is to understand the perceptions and lived experiences of children then it is vital to recognise and work with the knowledge that children already have, at least in experiential terms, of what it means to be a child:

> I am asking children, directly, to help me, an adult, to understand childhood. I want to investigate directly with the children ... I want to acquire from them their own unique knowledge ... I present myself as a person who, since she is an adult, does not have this knowledge. (2000:122)

The allegory of Antoine de Saint-Expéry's *The Little Prince* is useful in asserting that adults on their own cannot understand the world from the child's point of view, so need children to explain it to them. In our workshops it was very much this relationship that we sought to communicate. We explained that although we had seen the performances ourselves, we, as adults, wanted to know what *they*, as children and the people for whom the play was made thought. Cathy Malchiodi's articulates this relationship in terms of the researcher/therapist adopting a position of 'not knowing':

> By seeing the client as the expert on his or her own experiences, an openness to new information and discoveries naturally evolves for the therapist. Taking a stance of not knowing allows the child's experiences of creative and making art expression to be respected as individual and to have a variety of meanings. (1998:36)

The use of methodologically important techniques that ask participants to interpret their own data can also have ethical significance. It 'might be one step towards diminishing the ethical problems of imbalanced power relationships between research and researched at the point of data collection and analysis' (Morrow and Richards, 1996:100). The significance of this approach is the manner in which it continues the ongoing, mutually supportive relationship between questions of respect and good practice in research ethics with those of methodological and epistemological strength. In other words, the researcher's adoption of the attitude of 'not knowing' is both good ethical practice and good knowledge practice. Malchiodi's premise of 'not knowing', of perceiving the child as expert on his or her own art creations and experiences, is powerfully asserted and became an important methodological marker and aspiration for this research.

Ethical and participatory enquiry

The rationale behind the workshops, therefore, was that the children as research participants were engaged through drawing as a non-threatening and mediating activity via which their feelings and attitudes might be more revealingly communicated. Through such activities it may also be possible to explore aspects of an individual's experience that are unconscious or have gone unnoticed. Crucially, the next step was to ask participants in open, inquisitive and sometimes playful conversation, to reflect upon what they had drawn. In this way the research participants became the first and most important interpreters of the artefacts they created. Through the mediating, creative process, and the time this takes, the research was able to access the participants' reflective and engaged thoughts and responses, rather than only their instant or surface responses.

In this, the research also drew on concepts of participatory or co-operative enquiry, which asserts the value of working with people as fully engaged and informed individuals. Participatory methodologies seek to conduct research *with* individuals rather than *on* them, recognising and responding to the ethical and social responsibilities of conducting research involving people (Heron, 1996:19-35). With this in mind, the research workshops always began by explaining what we were doing and why. This was done briefly and in a manner that would not overwhelm or bemuse the participants. We also always provided further explanation if asked for by individual children. It has to be recognised that there are significant difficulties in conducting a fully parti-cipative piece of research with young children, particularly in terms of the school context where, as Morrow and Richards state, there is always a question over whether a child is ever in a position to dissent or not participate (1996: 101). So although obtaining the written consent of the children's guardians is essential and was the standard ethical procedure followed for the research described here, in terms of empowering the children it is largely ethically meaningless. It is certainly less important than the ongoing tacit negotiation of participation with the children themselves, which, as Hood, Kelley and Mayall describe, 'takes place not only before an interview, but *during* it' (original emphasis) (1996:124).

Our research did in fact differ also from another standard ethical practice in social research. Assurance of anonymity has become almost automatic, a position. It is assumed to be good practice, yet without reflection on the possible meanings and implications of anonymity. While anonymity is clearly vital in some research – especially to ensure safety or confidentiality – it disempowers the participants. Anonymity literally erases the actual people from the research results, and in some sense shifts ownership of their experiences and utterances to the expert and named researcher. My experience and that of other researchers also suggests that participants, particularly children, can resent or fail to understand the imposition of anonymity.

Unlike art therapy or work being conducted in the social services, my research was not seeking to explore sensitive or deeply personal issues through drawings or interviews but instead to reveal the children's responses to a piece of public theatre.

Consequently when we disseminated this research, including in a report document which we returned to all the participating schools, the children have their own first names. This means they are identifiable to themselves, although not to anybody else, as surnames and details of schools are not included. The children can retain ownership of their utterances and visual artefacts. At the end of the workshops we thanked the children for participating and asked their permission to reproduce and display their drawings and conversations. All the art works were then documented and the originals returned to the children. (For a useful discussion on this see Guenther, 2009).

Morrow and Richards suggest that in research with children it is necessary for 'respect' to become a methodological technique in itself (1996:101). It is hoped that the sensitive, caring, age appropriate, creative and fun methodologies adopted for this research fulfilled this objective. This is not, however, to elide the power imbalance that does still exist between researcher and researched and between adult and child – as Mayall puts it, 'a central characteristic of adults is that they have power over children' (2000:121) – but it hopes to address some of the manifestations of this imbalance.

Our methodology followed another tenet of participative enquiry: the importance of the participants themselves gaining something from the research process. This can take many forms, whether it is participants gaining a sense of self-knowledge, new skills or new perceptions. We hoped that the children involved in this project would gain a deeper response to the performance they had seen and a greater sense of their own experience. This did indeed happen and the workshops also provided a model to explore the use of drawing as a tool through which to increase and enhance children's engagement with their theatrical experiences. This is discussed further in Part Three.

However, the primary objective was that the participants would gain pleasure from taking part: pleasure from drawing, from the materials and time available to them, and pleasure from the attention and respect we awarded their pictures and experiences. Driven by such methodological concepts that rooted ethical, research and methodological practice, our objective was to run workshops that would be fun, participative and rewarding for the children, as well as useful for our research. The mediated and reflective responses provided by drawing, and talking about drawing, could be used to enable analysis and the in-depth description of how children respond to and remember their theatrical experiences.

Analysing the data

The material presented in the following chapters is drawn from a total of eleven visual arts workshops that took place following theatre performances. A total of 98 children from three primary schools in Edinburgh and West Lothian participated. The schools were selected according to the range of levels of theatre-going experience that the children could be expected to possess. In each instance, classes were selected to provide an audience of suitable age for the productions in question, with the workshops taking place as soon as possible after the children had attended the performance – some-times the same day, always within three days. The workshops were designed to explore the participants' responses to the particular performance they had seen, and the values, meanings and interpretations that they placed upon that recent experience. The result was the generation of an extraordinary rich and large amount of material, including over 250 drawings and paintings and over 40 hours of transcribed audio recordings.

While having the potential to produce tantalising insights into lived experience through its rich and varied texture, there remain serious questions about how to interpret and use this kind of data, not least because the sheer scale of the material makes it difficult to open up the methods and data to public inspection. Inevitably, any publication or report can only provide extracts and fragments of primary material as supporting evidence. One result of this can be, as David Silverman writes, that 'the critical reader is forced to ponder whether the researcher has selected only those fragments of data which support his argument' (1993:162).

The nature and character of any qualitative audience research also poses questions concerning the limits of wider application and generalisation. Although it is possible to make connections between the participants and a wider population, no direct demographic relationship exists, as would be the case with statistically weighted quantitative research. Additionally, while quantitative research tends to focus on the typical, the average or the majority, qualitative research of this nature highlights the particular, the context and the minutiae of concrete experiences. Such methods clearly have their limitations, suffering in terms of small sample sizes, lack of being truly representative and being inherently ambiguous.

One option is to respond by emphasising the particularities of the context, the representative limitations of the research and eschew all generalisations, instead celebrating the ethnographic richness of the material. Schoenmakers, for example, responds to the difficulty of expanding out from qualitative data to wider application by writing that

> Empirical research is not *per se* aiming at general propositions. A lot of empirical research in fact describes and documents audience participation and the reception of spectators at a special time and at a special place. (1990:102)

Similarly, Klein asserts the particularity of her empirical audience research, noting that 'conclusions inevitably reflect individual preference and aptitudes with regard to a specific performance rather than to speculations about the population at large or the theatre medium *per se*' (1987:10).

Yet at the same time such an attitude seems overly reticent and ignores the fact that, despite all cautions, anybody reading the material will develop their own generalisations and wider applications. As Geraghty states, the move to generalisation is 'entirely understandable ... academic work is after all concerned with making connections and testing out general propositions' (1998: 154). The analysis of the data presented in the following chapters seeks to do a little of both. It always starts with the particulars, and provides space to examine not just the typical responses amongst the children but also the exceptional and striking. It always begins with their experiences of the specific performances they watched. However, in presenting summaries and overviews it also invites wider application and introduces the possibility of reading out from the particular to the general. Readers will doubtless want to apply their own knowledge in pursuing and developing wider generalisations and I hope the richness of the material and the firm methodological grounding of the approach allows such readings to be made.

The methodological approach taken by any piece of research inevitably impacts on the nature of the material collected and the conclusions that can be drawn. As the methodology and processes of this creative audience research were particularly distinctive and challenging, it was important to explore them here in some detail. Hopefully the process is more than dry detailing of what was done and why. Methodology is process that 'shapes the nature of the conversation we can have with, and about, the world. Methodology is, in other words, the fundamental part of our story-telling technique' (Morrison, 1998:3). My discussion about researching the lived experience reveals much about the nature of the story about young audiences that is told in the following chapters.

5

Theatrical Illusion and
Material Reality

As Philip Pullman points out (page 15), the illusion of theatre is never complete:

> [Theatre] it has limitations. That isn't a real room, it's painted canvas, and it looks like it; that isn't a real boy, it's a little wooden puppet. But the limitations leave room for the audience to fill in the gaps. We pretend these things are real, so the story can happen.

The limitations in the ability of theatre to present a fully realised universe are particularly obvious when theatre is compared to film and television. With theatre there are always gaps between the material appearance of set, costumes, lighting and performers on the stage and the illusion they hope to communicate. The character of this relationship between reality and illusion can be wildly different in different productions, but a gap still exists. In his assertion that the spectator pretends that things on stage are real to allow the story to happen, Pullman is reiterating the familiar articulation of an audience's temporary suspension of disbelief and drawing our attention to that recurring question of the relationship between the theatrical illusion and the material reality of the production.

Swedish theatre researcher Willmar Sauter provides a useful construction of this relationship between reality and illusion, when he writes about the difference between the 'referential' and the 'embodied' experience of theatre (2000:191-5). The embodied experience relates to the actual appearance of a performance, the concrete appearance of stage flats, wooden puppets, lighting effects and so on. In this chapter I describe this as the experience of the *material reality* of a production. The referential experience is that which is described or evoked by the performance or, more colloquially, what an audience sees in their imagination. In the referential experience the stage flats become a landscape, the wooden puppet a real boy, the lighting the rising sun and so on. This I describe as the *evoked experience* of the theatrical illusion.

Sauter's concepts are particularly useful as they were formulated in the context of a piece of audience research looking into children's experiences of theatre, which will be discussed later in this chapter. Another writer who has engaged with this question is Jeanne Klein, who states:

> One of the biggest, ongoing myths about children's minds is that they have vast imaginations whereby they 'fill in' missing imagery on stage; however, the opposite tends to be true more often than not ... Child audiences are 'concrete' (literal) processors who focus on seeing the explicit visual images and hearing the explicit verbal dialogue presented to them. (2005:46)

Klein goes on to suggest that children begin to increase their ability to infer information from aspects not actualised on stage from around the age of eight. This, again, is something that will be explored in the following discussion.

To assist in unpacking such questions, this chapter explores children's responses to three different productions in terms of the relationship between their evoked and material experiences: or, in other words, whether the young audience responded to the illusion constructed by the performances (narrative, character, imagination) or to the material reality of the production (technique, skill, performance). In doing so it will map these discussions against the ideas of Pullman, Sauter and Klein, exploring what relationships exist between the experience, the illusion and the material reality of the stage.

Them With Tails – drawing the stories

The first of the productions I will discuss is *Them With Tails* by Tall Stories, which consists of two performers using improvisation, mime and slapstick to tell a series of mythical, fantastical stories. They do so with no set and minimal costumes or props. Almost nothing on the stage and almost everything is evoked through description and takes place in the imagination. Following these performances, six groups of children from two different schools participated in visual arts based research workshops, the details of which are discussed in the previous chapter.

In these workshops the first instruction we gave the children was to 'draw something you remember from the performance'. The immediate question that occurred to us was whether the children would draw what they literally saw: that is the material experience of two men standing on an almost bare stage. Or would they draw the stories: that is, the imagined or evoked experience of mermaids, magic fans, badgers, princesses, basilisks, clay pot boys and all the other things conjured up in the stories? The answer, with only a few exceptions, was that they drew the stories.

One of these exceptions is particularly interesting. Olimpia's drawing (figure 5.1) shows two men standing on a theatre stage, complete with lights running along the top. One man has some kind of pink tail; the other has a black tail and strange black headgear. The drawing includes some suitcases and boxes and three banners running vertically and horizontally. This is a fairly accurate depiction of the action at one moment in *Them With Tails*. Meanwhile Sophie, another child from the same school, drew precisely the same moment from the same production (figure 5.2). Sophie's drawing shows a woman with long blond hair, a pink dress and an extremely long, thin nose accompanied by a strange, small, black and white striped creature. They are in a wood. This again is an entirely accurate depiction of the action at that same moment.

The second child, Sophie, has drawn a moment from 'The Princess and the Badger', a story about a badger, a princess and a magic fan that had the ability to make people's noses grow longer or shorter depending which side of the face was fanned. Sophie, like the vast majority of the children, has drawn the story as realised in her imagination. She has depicted things that never appeared on stage but were just described or alluded to. As it happened, the first child, Olimpia, was a Polish girl who had recently joined the school and who understood little English. When she saw the production, therefore, she had absolutely no idea what the stories were about and could only draw the physical appearance of what she saw on the stage. With no alternative, she drew the material experience.

Of 132 pictures of *Them With Tails* produced as free drawings, Olimpia's was one of only seven that depicted the production in a material rather than evoked fashion. A further six mixed the material and evoked experience, while five were unclear. These raw numbers are striking and revealing, demonstrating how most of the children drew either complete scenes or specific moments from the production or pictures that concentrated on showing the appearance of a single character. However, there are various reasons, including group influences and the dynamics of the drawing pro-

Figure 5.1: Drawing the Material Experience: 'The Princess and the Badger' by Olimpia

Figure 5.2: Drawing the Evoked Experience: 'The Princess and the Badger' by Sophie

cess, that tell us we should be cautious about the value of counting or content analysis techniques in this context. Instead, it is through the subtler relationship between conversations and drawings that a fuller sense of the children's experiences emerges.

Exceptions are always interesting, and a small number of children were more inclined to draw what they saw. One of these was Callum, who drew a man in a crown-like hat, holding two feathers in his outstretched hands (figure 5.3). Callum was a boy who did not want to talk a great deal, limiting his description of this drawing to it being of 'the chicken guy', whom he liked 'cos he was funny'. In one interesting exchange, a girl in Callum's class criticised his drawing:

> **Megan**: That isn't a chicken.
>
> **Researcher**: Now I actually disagree with you Megan because I think it does look like what Callum saw. Because what have you drawn here Callum? [Callum is silent; there is a pause]
>
> **Megan**: I get it.
>
> **Researcher**: What do you think it is   Megan that he's drawn?
>
> **Megan**: It's a person dressed up in a costume.

What Callum had drawn is in fact the material experience of a basilisk that appeared in one of the stories. Not surprisingly, none of the children knew what a basilisk – presented in the production as a cross between a bird and a snake – was supposed to look like. When faced with depicting something they did not fully understand, the children sometimes responded by ignoring it, at other times by latching onto what they did recognise and making that the centre of their interpretation. So in this instance a number of the children latched onto what they did know and transformed the basilisk into a kind of monstrous chicken. Callum's picture, however, is pretty much what he saw: as Megan puts it, 'a person dressed up in a costume'. The precise reasons behind his choices in how to draw this image are largely inaccessible, particularly as, although a willing drawer, he had no interest in discussing his pictures.

In response to *Them With Tails*, therefore, most of the children drew something relating to the evoked experience of the production: they drew the stories, seeking to depict either a moment in the action or a detail of a character. There is something very compelling in such responses, which show us that these children engaged with the production in a manner that allowed them to complete the gaps within their imaginations. Such a perception would no doubt delight the production team and many adults who might desire to celebrate children's imaginative engagement with theatre.

Figure 5.3: 'The Chicken Guy' in *Them With Tails* by Callum

These results might suggest that, at some level and for some of the children, the actual performance became, if not forgotten, then partly suppressed in favour of the imaginative experience. But this is too simplistic as the children's ongoing conversations indicated that they engaged with the production on several levels. While often beginning through relation of narrative or character, their conversations were multilayered and could be characterised as possessing a duality of vision: seeing and remembering both the material and the evoked at the same time. This is suggested in an exchange between one researcher and Ruaridh, discussing a drawing of a monkey up a tree:

> **Researcher**: Um, tell me how the monkey looks, what does the monkey look like?
>
> **Ruaridh**: He looks like, he looks brown and he has a tail, a tiny tail and big brown fur but it wasn't really in the story.
>
> **Researcher**: What was he like in the, in the one that you saw then?
>
> **Ruaridh**: Skin, skin and um, and a fake, a little tail, and...
>
> **Researcher**: Did the man do anything that made him look like a monkey?
>
> **Ruaridh**: Just the tail.
>
> **Researcher**: But you knew he was a monkey?
>
> **Ruaridh**: Yeah I knew he was a monkey but I knew he wasn't really a monkey, I just knew that he was playing as a monkey.

Asked what the monkey looked like, Ruaridh describes a real monkey, which is what he drew, but immediately adds the description of how the monkey was staged. In his conversation, so presumably in his memory, the evoked and imagined experience is always accompanied by the seen and material experience – and vice versa. The two are mutually entangled. That this duality existed in the children's verbally articulated memories but was not manifested to the same extent in their drawings is interesting. It certainly means that we cannot say that they did not notice or remember the artifice and material experience. Perhaps instead it suggests that they knew perfectly well what it was that they were *supposed* to be paying attention to and had accepted that convention actively and positively. So later the conversation above continues:

> **Researcher**: So are you going to put the monkey on the tree?
>
> **Ruaridh**: Yeah but going to make it look like a real monkey.

Ruaridh in other words knew that the alternative choice would have been to draw the fake monkey, the man monkey, but that was an option he clearly never truly considered.

The conclusion of this chapter reflects on some of these points. First, it is worth comparing the aspects observed in relation to *Them With Tails* with the responses provoked by the two very different productions seen by children taking part in the project, *Martha* and *Psst!*, both of which featured puppets. The children's responses to these puppets naturally became a focal point for interpretation. Appropriately, this immediately raises key questions about how young audiences respond to different levels of theatrical illusion and the skills and strategies they use to follow, understand, and interpret the performance.

Puppets, illusion and reality

Writing in the 1930s, Paul McPharlin articulates what is perhaps the classic sentiment about how audiences respond to puppets:

> When puppets come alive ... one ceases to think of wood and wire; one is absorbed in the action.... The audience, accepting the convention of puppets, projects itself into them with the same empathy that it feels for any other actors. (cited in Tillis, 1992:47)

However, while such assertions are customary, the nature of actual lived experiences and perceptions is far less clear and seldom investigated. Do audiences watching live theatre really respond to a wooden puppet with the same empathy as they would to a real boy? Or, to frame the question more widely, do audiences respond to the illusion or to the material reality of puppets in a theatre performance? The focus on puppets in this chapter is partly expedient but also deliberate, as they render the gap between the stage reality and the evoked illusion explicit and transparent.

Otakar Zich's discussion of the possible ways in which an audience might respond to puppets (1923) is widely discussed. Zich proposed that 'the puppets may be perceived as living people or as lifeless dolls' (cited in Bogatyrev, 1983:48-49). He elaborates on these alternatives: on the one hand, the uncanny wonder of puppets coming to life and, on the other, of the grotesque and comic response to the attempt to feign life with lifeless dolls. Scott Cutler Shershow charts this dualism of aesthetic effect thus:

Unreal	Real
Inanimate (merely material)	Animate (illusion of life)
Grotesque and comic	Mysterious and wondrous
(Shershow, 1995:215)	

Zich effectively articulates the recurring question about the audience's perception of puppets, which is why commentators return to his writing. But it is also fundamentally flawed and limited, not least in the assertion that these are mutually exclusive categories of perception 'since we can perceive [puppets] *only* one way at a time'.

This position is challenged by Steve Tillis, who proposes instead that, far from being antithetical, a simultaneous acknowledgement of the puppet's two aspects is amongst the defining characteristics of their perception. Tillis describes a 'double vision' whereby an audience sees the puppet both as an object and as a life, each aspect inescapable at the same moment as they are contradictory. He describes this constant tension as one of the key pleasures of puppet theatre, since 'the puppet pleasurably challenges its audience's understanding of what it means to be an 'object' and what it means to have a 'life" (1992:64).

Another difficulty with Zich's position is that it is ideologically loaded. This becomes more apparent in Henryk Jurkowski's extrapolation from Zich:

> we recognize in his descriptions the perceptions of two kinds of publics: the folk audience's perception (puppets are mysterious) and the erudite audience's perception (puppets are puppets). (1983:124)

Shershow rightly points out the class implications of this construction, which celebrates the instinctive responses of the uneducated 'folk' at the same time as asserting that they are essentially unsophisticated and uninformed. In other words, the perception of puppets as real, mysterious and wondrous is charming and earthy yet essentially wrong. In contrast, the perception of puppets as unreal and grotesquely comic in their attempt to animate the inanimate is knowing, sophisticated and correct.

This hierarchical and power loaded dualism is replicated in constructions of the relationship between child and adult audiences. Petr Bogatyrev, for example, articulates the commonplace perception that 'children's perception of puppet theater undoubtedly differs strongly from that of adults' (1983:62). His argument is essentially that children will perceive puppets as 'real', responding in a manner that is wondrous and instinctive, while in contrast adults may well respect the skills constructing the illusion but will always compare the puppet to the human actor and see its representational limitations.

For Bogatyrev, the primary reason for this would be levels of experience and semiotic competence; while Shershow suggests that such responses are produced by children being 'born into a social world in which certain practices have already been designated as childish or mature, simple or sophisticated'

(1995:223). In other words, the response is a kind of learnt behaviour, produced by a society that expects children to respond to the magic and wonder of puppets, whereas adults learn that their supposedly mature and sophisticated perception requires them to see through the illusion.

Left entirely unexplored is children's own lived experiences and how they relate to an ideological and power-loaded classification of perception. So how do these debates about the nature of an audience's perception of puppets relate to the research conducted into children's actual theatrical experiences?

Psst! – puppets or people?

Psst!, by Danish company Teatre Refleksion, is a piece of intimate puppet theatre that features a ballerina, jugglers, clowns and various other characters, all represented by a variety of puppets. Most are handheld, such as two clowns whose heads are formed by small balls held on the end of short rods and their bodies and legs by the gloved hands of the puppeteer. Another puppet is a long-limbed, curly-haired ballerina, whose jointed arms and legs are held directly in the fingers of two puppeteers working in tandem. The only exception to these handheld puppets is a character that returns in three or four interludes between the action and moves via an unseen mechanism along grooves in the stage floor. Only during its appearances are the puppeteers not fully visible on stage: since they wear elaborate white costumes and hats, the puppeteers are always much in evidence.

The puppets speak no dialogue and, although the production includes loose narrative threads about characterisation, a love story and the circus setting, it is primarily driven by episodic scenes and by the puppets' appearance and abilities. At the end of the performance the children are invited to the front of the stage and allowed to handle the puppets and talk to the puppeteers. We took a class of 23 six to seven year olds to see this production and held three visual arts workshops afterwards to explore the children's experiences. We asked them, as with all the workshops, to draw something they remembered from the production.

Looking at the children's drawings of *Psst!* it is immediately noticeable that there are very few pictures featuring the puppeteers, even though they were visible at all times. Neither is there anything indicating that the little people they drew were puppets at all. Of the 52 pictures produced through free drawing, only five feature the puppeteers in some form or other, and none of these does so unambiguously. The remaining 47 drawings depict a variety of little people with no indication that these characters were actually puppets.

Figure 5.4: The puppets as people by Michael

Michael's drawing (figure 5.4) is typical: he shows the puppets as people, with complete legs, hands and other details which certainly were not to be seen in the performance.

As with the initial examination of the drawings of *Them With Tails*, therefore, the immediate impression is that in their recollection of the performance the children have neglected what we might call the reality or material experience of the theatre in favour of depicting the character and action of the evoked experience. The validity of this initial impression is developed in a moment, particularly in relation to the children's conversations that accompanied their drawings. First, however, it is helpful to relate these responses to a piece of research described by Sauter in *The Theatrical Event* (2000) that has many striking parallels.

Comparison with *The Lonely Ear*

In this book Sauter presents a discussion of some audience research conducted into a puppet show for children aged three to five years old called *The Lonely Ear*. It was performed in Sweden in the 1990s by Michael Meschke. Sauter describes the complex layering of the production: at several points the puppeteer addressed the audience directly and talked about the puppets, which the children were allowed to handle for themselves afterwards. Sauter also notes the 'obvious artificiality' of performance and how on a sensory level – speaking we must suppose from the perspective of himself as an adult observer – the puppeteer dominated the production. The research into the reception of *The Lonely Ear* included participant observation and drawings, and therefore has direct parallels with the research conducted with *Psst!*, both in terms of methodology and the form and appearance of the production.

And, as with the children's initial responses to *Psst!*, most of the children's drawings of the Swedish production 'neglect the reality of the theatre' in favour of representing character and action. Sauter observes that

> In their perception of the performance, most children neglected the reality of the theatre – the puppeteer, the technique, the props – and concentrated literally on the 'building of the character.' Despite their consciousness of the theatrical process during the performance, they felt free to transpose the embodied into the referential. (2000:195)

In his analysis of responses to *The Lonely Ear*, Sauter places particular stress on this because of the audience's necessary awareness of the material reality of the performance. Necessary in this instance not only because it was transparently there – the puppeteer was visible throughout – but also because the

production self-referentially drew attention to the nature of its own construction and broke any fourth wall barrier with the audience, through directly
addressing the audience, having them handle the puppets and so on.

With *Psst!*, the puppeteers were similarly always visible to the audience. Here
too the puppets were at times constructed in full view, their artificiality made
transparent and here too the audience were invited to handle them at the
end. In all these aspects the material reality of the performance would seem
to dominate on a sensory level and yet in the drawings of both *Psst!* and *The
Lonely Ear* it is the evoked experience that dominates. This would seem to
confirm Petr Bogatyrev's assertion that

> The signs of puppet theatre predominate, precisely when there is an audience
> of children, and therefore puppet theatre achieves its maximum expressive-
> ness with this audience. [Conversely] with adult audiences, the signs of theater
> with live actors dominate the perception of puppet theatre. (cited in Shershow,
> 1995:223)

As an adult, Sauter felt that the live presence of the puppeteer dominated the
perception of *The Lonely Ear*, but for the children it was the puppets themselves
that dominated. What is presumed here is a description of the immediate and
wondrous nature of the child audience perception, which is charming but at
the same time unsophisticated and theatrically illiterate.

I believe, however, that this analysis of these child responses is incomplete.
There is not enough data available for me to interrogate the responses to *The
Lonely Ear* any further. In particular, I do not have access to the children's
verbal explication of their own drawings, nor indeed do I know if this vital
stage in the analysis was carried out. In relation to *Psst!*, however, a more
sustained investigation into the responses casts doubt on the completeness
of the children's transformation of the material into the evoked. In particular,
it is worth remembering the methodological discussion in Chapter Four
about analysing drawings as evidence in isolation. Here it is necessary to
match the drawings to the children's conversation, with the result that a much
more ambiguous and multi-layered impression emerges.

The drawings and the dialogue

That the children overwhelmingly drew the puppets as people perhaps
affirms the popular perception of the powerful imaginations of young children and their willingness to accept illusion as reality. However, it should not
be taken as suggesting that the children did not notice or appreciate the
material reality of the performance. When asked about this directly, they

frequently asserted that their drawings were of puppets and that anybody looking at the drawings *would see puppets*:

Researcher: Would they say they were people?

Fraser: These are puppets.

Researcher: And they could tell they were puppets?

Fraser: Because we drew them very good.

As we have seen that only in a few instances do the drawings accurately represent the puppets *as puppets*. In contrast, their conversations refute the possibility that the children's perceptions neglected the reality of the theatre. In the following exchange, for example, it is noticeable how readily Robert answers the questions about how the puppets work, but has little interest in possible narratives or characterisation (see figure 5.5).

Figure 5.5: Puppets from *Psst!* by Robert.
The matching figures top and centre are the clowns. The figure at the centre bottom and far right is the 'Wee Rascal', discussed below, who moved along grooves in the stage, which Robert has represented here as lines. The figure on the left is a performer playing cat's cradles.

Researcher: So these were the two puppets [pointing at the middle two figures], can you remember how they worked?

Robert: Em, yeah, em, the person was holding their body with a wee stick coming from their head so they could, em, like make them jump and make their head come off.

Researcher: And then they had legs and hands as well, and they've got hats with bells on. Why do they have hats with bells on?

Robert: I don't know, they just had them on them.

Researcher: And do you think they were doing anything in particular or were they...?

Robert: I don't know what they were doing.

Researcher: Did it matter that you didn't know what they were doing?

Robert: No.

Clearly Robert was very aware of the workings of the puppets, which seemed to engage the children's attention in recollection far more than the imaginative or narrative aspects of the production. In the exchange above it is noticeable that Robert is uninterested in talking about the puppets' status as clowns or in even thinking about what they were doing as characters or within the narrative. It is possible that this was a result of limitations in the production, with these aspects simply not strong enough to grasp Robert's attention. Alternatively, engagement with the technical and material aspects of the performance can be read as a *positive* engagement, valued in its own right.

Interest in the mechanical workings of the puppets was particularly noticeable in the instance where a puppet moved without the visible assistance of a puppeteer (see again figure 5.5). All the children, although particularly the boys, enjoyed speculating on how this puppet moved, suggesting magnets, remote control, string, a person under the stand, a stick and much else. Several of the children included in their drawings lines representing the slits along which this puppet moved. Another boy elaborated, producing a cutaway image of what might be below the stage.

It is revealing that this technical engagement into how the puppet worked was accompanied by or perhaps actively motivated several of the boys to be significantly more interested, imaginatively and emotionally, in this character. They imagined dialogue for the character to say or created short stories or explanations about what it was doing, thus taking the action further in their imagination than the elements afforded them by the performance. And whereas none of the puppets were named in the production, in the workshops this character, but only this one, was named by the children. Other figures were given descriptors, such as the acrobats, the ballerina or the fat man. But this character was given the name the 'Wee Rascal' by one group, because it came out at night and crept slyly about, and the two other groups named it 'Mr Bean' – because 'he' hummed to himself in a manner similar to the cartoon version of Mr Bean. Two boys went on to transform this into 'Super Mr Bean' and the character engaged in a whole series of mini-adventures played out on paper.

The freedom and playfulness with which the children were able to engage with the 'Wee Rascal' was striking, particularly because it combined consciousness of the theatrical process – that is, awareness and reflection on the manner of the puppet's construction – and the freedom to transform, extend and play with this in other worlds and other spaces. In other words, engagement with the technical or material experience of this character offered an alternative route for engagement, one that particularly appealed to the boys.

Whether gender was a significant factor in the children's engagement with theatre is not a central aspect of this study. As should be expected, there was as much variation in response within each gender as between genders. Nonetheless, looking at the material discussed here it is possible that boys were somewhat more frequently engaged than girls with the material or technical experience of a production. With *Psst!* it was the boys who mostly produced technical representations or responses to the performances, including set plans and cut away models that revealed the hidden workings of a production underneath the stage. Girls and boys noticed the same things but they found different elements interesting and worth developing.

In a culture where boys are increasingly struggling within school settings, particularly in arts subjects, the suggestion that boys and girls have broadly different perceptual experiences with theatre is significant. We should be aware that there may be a tendency to term girls' engagement with the referential experience as 'correct', as it often complies with the adult's hoped for response. But we should celebrate the nature of boys' engagement too, and use the processes of theatrical illusion, rather than the illusion itself, as a way of engaging their technical creativity.

Balancing layers of perception

While the drawings largely communicate one level of perception, that of the evoked experience, the children's conversations demonstrate a more nuanced and sophisticated balancing of several layers of perception – seeing and responding to both the material and the evoked at the same time. In the end we can only speculate as to why the children's drawings of *Psst!* seemed overwhelmingly to neglect the reality of the theatre. One likely possibility is that the children had a clear grasp of the cultural rules of representation – they were aware that they were *supposed* to engage with the evoked, imaginative experience of the puppets. It is also possible that there is something about the nature of drawing as a medium that encouraged one form of representation, while conversation elicited another.

Overall, however, it is clear that the children were simultaneously aware of the material and evoked aspects of a production in a manner that contradicts Zich's suggestion that such modes of perception are mutually exclusive. Instead, the responses more closely match Tillis' concept of 'double vision' in that the children attended to the puppet in two ways at once. And in the children's responses their engagement with and appreciation of the technical experience actively enhanced and supported their imaginative investment in the production. This supports Tillis' argument that audiences obtain pleasure from the complex relationship between object and life presented within the puppet performance. Expanding this concept out beyond puppet theatre, Anne Ubersfeld writes that audiences gain pleasure from the multifold nature of the experience:

> it is the pleasure of an absence being summoned up (the narrative, the fiction, elsewhere); and it is the pleasure of contemplating a stage reality experienced as a concrete activity in which the spectator takes part (1982:128)

Such contradictory responses – believing and disbelieving; engagement with the craft of making and with the illusion itself – mark the presence of what I believe to be a fairly sophisticated theatrical competence. These may well be inexperienced, uninformed and indisputably childlike audience members, but they can accept contradictions, can give in to the illusion and take pleasure in theatrical technique at the same time. This is a point that can be developed further by exploring how slightly older children responded in both referential and embodied manners to the puppet goose featured in *Martha*.

Martha and the Goose

Martha, by Catherine Wheels Theatre Company, is a fairly traditional narrative-driven production. In contrast to *Them With Tails* or *Psst!*, it possesses strong elements of naturalistic presentation, including sustained characters and chronological plotting. The narrative is essentially about Martha, a lonely and angry woman who is befriended by a charming and irascible goose played by a puppet. The goose eventually has to follow its instincts and fly away on migration, but through the meeting Martha learns of the benefits and rewards of friendship. The production is staged on a carefully detailed and naturalistic set, featuring Martha's ramshackle house and other details of the beach setting.

Martha provided many of the details that the two other productions left to the audience's imagination. Nonetheless, significant gaps existed between the extent of this presentation and the illusion evoked. For example, while the house was three-dimensional and full of detail, it was roofless; while the beach was painted yellow and littered with flotsam, it was clearly sandless; while the goose was brilliantly manipulated, full-scale and full of character, it was clearly a puppet with glued on feathers, glass eyes, wheels and controlling rods sticking out of its head and back.

Twenty children from one class of nine to ten year olds took part in two visual arts workshops after seeing *Martha*, which was performed in their school hall. They were three to four years older than those who saw *Psst!* and, along

Figure 5.6: The goose flying by Jordan

with correspondingly more developed drawings, there were other distinctions in their responses. While with *Psst!* the children's drawings, if not their conversations, overwhelmingly appeared to render the puppets as real people, with *Martha* the situation was more evenly divided. The goose was drawn by almost all the children at some point in the workshops: 23 of the 39 pictures produced through free drawing featured the goose in one form or another. Of these, nine were drawings where the goose is represented in a broadly real fashion, with wings or feathers or flying (as in figure 5.6). In these, the children have drawn what was evoked for them by the staging and the narrative, completing the mental picture and making concrete the referential perspective in their drawings.

In ten other instances, however, the goose is depicted, broadly speaking, as a puppet, drawn accurately to its literal appearance, complete with wheels, controlling sticks and even, in most cases, a puppeteer (see figure 5.7). In these drawings the children have depicted the material experience, drawing what they saw and reproducing the reality of the stage performance.

The children thus produced both literal depictions of what was seen and imaginative representations of what was evoked. The most immediate explanation for this might be the age of the children, who at nine and ten were beginning to move from childhood into adolescence, with a concomitant shifting mode of perception from that of wonder and belief to one of increasing knowledge. In Zich's formulation these are mutually exclusive modes of perception and the almost equal division of their drawings perhaps signifies these children's position on the cusp between these two ages and two modes of perception.

Appreciating the technique

However, these modes of perception are not incompatible. In some of their drawings the children attend to both the referential and the embodied at same time, depicting things as seen and things as imagined within a single frame. Additionally, the conversations that accompanied the drawings reveal that part of the pleasure for the children was being able to recognise how the character and emotion of the goose was created through the artifice of the puppet.

So, for example, several children drew the goose with wheels – ie as a puppet – but depicted it in a very expressive posture – ie as a character. Moreover, the children were interested in talking about how they had perceived these emotions in the puppet:

Researcher: So did the goose have different expressions sometimes during the show?

Ronan: Yes, it wasn't on his face. It was just like like when he was sad he had his head down.

As in this exchange, the recognition and appreciation of the technique used to manipulate and present the puppet goose recurred time and again in the children's talk, and was reflected in the children's materially correct and technical drawings of the puppet. The children appreciated these techniques

Figure 5.7: The goose as a puppet by Rory

because of the effect produced, and when they chose to depict the goose as a puppet it was often as a puppet full of expressive force. This is an example of how the children engaged with the goose in two ways: as a character that they imaginatively completed as a real goose; and as a puppet, which they engaged with in terms of how it was operated.

When asked directly whether they were watching the goose or the man, most children said the goose. Of course they were clearly looking at both, and indeed were perhaps aware that the 'correct' thing to say to this question was 'goose':

> **Researcher**: And did you look at him or did you look at the goose?
>
> **Rory**: Look at both of them.
>
> **Researcher**: And do you think you were supposed to look at him or look at the goose?
>
> **Rory**: Goose.

As this boy was aware, it would be the intention of the theatre company that the audience look at the goose. This is, moreover, the 'correct' answer in being the one that adults desire from children – if it were otherwise most people would feel that something was not working in the production. After all, as implied earlier by McPharlin, you are not supposed to notice the manipulation, but to buy into the illusion of the puppet. This is implicitly but dramatically demonstrated by the production photographs of *Martha* offered online by the theatre company; each image features Martha and the goose, but none reveal more than the hands of the puppeteer. The emphasis is clearly on the character and emotional reality of the goose.

The range of imaginative responses

With theatre, not all the information or representation appears on the stage; much is left to the audience's imagination. Indeed, in many instances the audience is required to use their imagination to make sense of the production. As a production, *Martha* provided a stage picture that was quite naturalistically detailed; the set, the costumes, the sound effects and so on were all present and directed towards providing a full sensory experience. Nonetheless, the puppet clearly required completing through the imagination, as did a variety of other elements.

The children certainly could produce beautiful drawings that completed the evoked experience and depicted a fully realised referential narrative of *Martha*. For example, Zoe (figure 5.8) was one of three children who produced drawings that captured a moment only experienced in the imagination, when Martha's goose joins its family and flies away at the end of the production. In performance, this moment was constructed through sound effects and textual indicators pointing towards an off-stage migration.

On paper these children's drawings are fantastically evocative depictions of this imagined experience, which the children have completed through their artwork. There is something very compelling in these pictures. They show us that the children were fully engaged with the production in a manner that allowed them to complete the spaces within their own imaginations; it is tempting to celebrate these responses. I suggest that this level of imaginative engagement, although no doubt present during and inspired by the production, was partly brought into being through the task of drawing itself. When asked to draw, the children were often required to do more than depict what they saw. They had to make choices, add and invent detail, provide context and background and, in doing so, were transforming, extending and possessing the experience. The role of drawing in extending children's experience of live theatre is something I have been developing in conjunction with Imaginate and is explored in detail in Chapter Nine.

Not that these drawings should be valued over others that depict the goose as seen; they provide just as richly textured a depiction yet just happen to include the puppeteer. To do so seems falsely to demarcate the boundaries of the legitimate response to a production and to limit the nature of theatrical engagement.

> Rick Conte, the puppeteer in *Martha*, provides a lovely anecdote about how the children in the audience see both the puppet and the puppeteer. At one point in the play Martha complainingly remarks, 'There's a goose in the house', at which point in one performance a boy in the audience shouts out, 'Aye, and a man too!' The brilliance of this is that the shouted remark is absolutely within the traditions of appropriate child participation, but the observation is more familiar to that of stand-up comedy.

We might speculatively construct all sorts of reasons why the children who saw *Martha* were split fairly evenly between drawing the puppet and drawing the goose. These include the children's age: some might have felt that the production or puppets in general was a little babyish for them; for several it translated into an increased interest in figuring out how things worked and

Figure 5.8: The geese flying away by Zoe

wanting to produce technical drawings; and for others it might have resulted from an increased emphasis on literal accuracy in drawing. One result was certain: the children simultaneously engaged in both the illusion and reality of the performance and of the puppet, demonstrating their ability to read the production on two levels simultaneously.

Significantly, the goose was not the only aspect of the production that produced this dual response of accepting the illusion and enjoying being able to perceive how it was achieved. The children talked in similar ways about the sound effects and set design, the acting and voice, as well as the puppet. It is possible that children's literal, technical and intellectual responses to theatre are as important – and in their way as creative – as their emotional or imaginative engagement with narrative or character. They might be neglected as undesirable by adults who wish children to remain children – and dogmatically only see the illusion – but this ability to hold both the fact and the fiction in mind at the same time marks the beginning of a truly sophisticated relationship with theatre and art.

Noticing the reality – completing the illusion

In his discussion of children's theatre experiences, Willmar Sauter suggests that children's imaginative engagement with a performance means that, even when explicitly introduced to the technical or material aspects of the production, they nonetheless primarily draw theatre – and by implication primarily experience it – in terms of the evoked. In terms of semiotic and theoretical understanding, such responses fit neatly into the expected child-like perceptions of puppets in live theatre presented by Zich, Bogatyrev and others.

At times in the examples presented in this chapter this certainly did occur, particularly if the children's drawings are considered in isolation from their conversations. In response to both *Psst!* and *Martha*, many of the children produced drawings depicting the evoked experience, representing the puppets as animate, wondrous and real. Similarly with *Them With Tails,* it is the narratives, characters, imagined settings and evoked costumes that are prominent and fully realised in the drawings. There is a temptation to celebrate this as a triumph for both the productions and the richness of children's imaginations.

Yet such a response also sustains an effective disempowerment of children by ignoring the complexity and sophistication of their perception. Peter Brook, amongst others, has articulated the sophistication of supposedly naïve 'folk' audiences and, in doing so, has sought to return power and ownership to such audiences, their responses no longer being perceived as naïve, illiterate or passive but instead active and engaged. Something similar applies to children's responses, where assertions about protecting the magic of theatre for children by not destroying the illusion are in effect disempowering actions that use adult authority to underestimate and patronise children. For when considering the children's conversations alongside their drawings, it is evident that the children saw, remembered and were interested in both the material and evoked aspects of the productions.

For Zich the two broad categories of perception – seeing the puppet or seeing the illusion – were incompatible. The material presented in the paper suggests that for children and probably for adults too this is far from the case. In response to *Martha*, the children were able to invest fully in the character of the goose, and at the same time notice, appreciate and engage with the manners through which this character was created. Moreover, engagement with the one enhanced the other.

This affirms the concept put forward by both Tillis and Ubersfeld of an audience's 'double vision' and pleasure in a dual reading of the production which oscillates between attending to the real and the imagined. The tension, indeed the power, of the experience resides in the balance between faith and doubt. In a different realm, one familiar cultural example that occurs to me is children's relationship with the story of Father Christmas. My own anecdotal experience suggests that this often resides in a fluctuating position of belief and disbelief, faith and suspicion. The continued balance between these positions, rather than assertion of certainty in one or another, seems to me to be a radical, liminal and perceptually sophisticated act.

I am not saying that we should want children either literally or metaphorically to draw the puppeteer, to see only the material appearance and ignore the illusion; that we should not want children to lose themselves in the magic of the experience. I am saying rather that the well-meaning desire to protect the magic of the illusion for children is ill-serving and can be patronising. Children have the ability to juggle contradicting interpretations and to see simultaneously on two levels. This ability allows them to pursue and preserve the magic of the illusion if they desire, but to do so in an empowered and enfranchised manner.

It is easy to delight in the ability of children to immerse themselves in the evoked experience. I want to stress that we should also celebrate their technical engagement with the embodied experience. In engaging with theatre as theatre, they are perceiving the workings of the medium itself and appreciating the illusion that is produced; they are following not just the story but also the processes of the construction of the story.

Pullman asserts the necessity of audiences working with theatre to complete the illusion and compensate for the limitations of the form. This is certainly true and present in the children's responses discussed here. But as well as the audience working *for* the production, the sophisticated spectator also appreciates the work *of* the production – the craft, technique and struggle that goes into constructing the illusion. To be lost in the moment at the same time as consciously watching the construction of that moment is an immensely complicated and immensely rewarding piece of mental self-trickery; simultaneous belief and disbelief.

6

Theatrical Competence

This chapter explores the broad theme of the children's competences and perceptions when it comes to watching theatre. At its simplest, this asks whether children have the intellectual and emotional resources to interpret and appreciate or to 'get' the performances they watch. How developed, flexible and refined are young children's skills of perception and theatrical literacy? Inevitably the answers will be determined by the particular children and particular productions engaged with in this research, although, as elsewhere, the reader is invited to extend or modify the discussion in light of their own experiences and observations.

The concept of theatrical competence itself is worth considering briefly. As Bernard Rosenblatt puts it, theatrical literacy 'requires the ability to perceive, recognise and interpret dramatic symbol systems at various intellectual levels' (cited in Klein 1987:9). Connected to this central question is whether such ability to 'read' the stage varies according to age, theatre-going experience or other social factors. This can also be considered in terms of Pierre Bourdieu's concept of cultural capital:

> A work of art has meaning and interest only for someone who possesses the cultural competence, that is, the code, into which it is encoded. [...] A beholder who lacks the specific code feels lost in a chaos of sounds and rhythms, colours and lines, without rhyme or reason. (1984:3)

As Bourdieu describes it, responses to art involve a conscious and unconscious decoding operation where the viewer or reader's response is determined by the capital – the knowledge, skills, experience, background – that he or she brings to the work. 'The capacity to see', writes Bourdieu, 'is a function of knowledge' (1984:2). In part, therefore, this chapter will explore what knowledge is required for children to 'decode' a theatrical performance, bearing in mind that elements of this are likely to be assumed within our society. As the chapter develops this question will also shift, considering whether young children have a sense of their own abilities of theatrical competence.

Aspects of this debate have already been anticipated by some of the discussion in the previous chapter relating to children's ability to read theatrical illusion. Here, however, this key issue will be explored explicitly, first in relation to *Them With Tails* and then to *Martha* and *Psst!*

Signs to signification

Philip Pullman's remarks are again useful here: 'the very limitations of theatre allow the audience to share in the acting. In fact they require the audience to pretend. It won't work if they don't'. With a production such as *Them With Tails*, which was driven by verbal storytelling, the 'limitations of theatre' are its inability to show the stories to the audience in a fully realised manner – in the manner, for instance, of a Disney or Pixar animation. Instead the stories are illustratively told to the audience, who are then required to complete them within their own imaginations.

Pullman therefore reminds us that the audience is required to work with theatre, to lend their engagement and imagination, in order to make it complete. The previous chapter explored how after watching *Them With Tails*, rather than draw what they had literally seen – two men on an almost bare stage – the children instead drew fully realised representations of the stories and characters. At a fundamental level, this fact explicitly reveals that the children had the ability and competence to 'get' the performance – they were working with the production and the production was working for them.

In his analysis of children's drawings of theatre performances, discussed in the previous chapter, Willmar Sauter reaches a similar conclusion. Asking if small children can follow the complicated sensory, artistic and symbolic levels of a performance, his primary criteria is whether they are able to construct 'references in relation to what they perceived as embodied action' – in other words if they could extrapolate from the literal staged action to the evoked references. He concludes that they certainly could. Their drawings demonstrated clearly that the children 'had understood' the theatrical presentation' (2000:195).

So, for example, in response to *Them With Tails* Nasra drew a particular scene from one of the stories. Here a wolf-like creature stands on a rock in a river or pond, looking down at a crocodile lying in the water below and blowing bubbles. In conversation Nasra related the story behind her picture:

Researcher: What happened in the story?

Nasra: That thing wanted to ... the crocodile wanted to trick him but he tricked the crocodile.

Researcher: And what was the crocodile's plan?

Nasra: To blow the bubbles and think that he's, that he's the crab and then he'll think ... and then he knew that it wasn't the crab, he knew it was the crocodile.

None of this was actually visible on the stage; instead it was evoked through description and mime. Nasra, however, has not limited herself to recounting the concrete stage performance, but has constructed from such embodied action a detailed imaginating of one particular moment in a complex and convoluted story.

This is an example of how children transform the material fact of the performance – that is, what they saw on the stage – into the referential – that is, what was evoked by the performance or, more colloquially, what they saw in their mind's eye. The facility with which the children did this demonstrates that they completely *got* the performance. If they had been unable to understand the theatrical presentation they could not have produced these drawings (as, for example, in the case of Olimpia, who lacked the *linguistic* competence to understand the performance). From this general level of understanding, we are able to explore how the children decoded assumed but extremely complex theatrical languages: understanding the conventions of staging, the use of symbols and signs to stand in for the whole, the difference between an actor and a character, the storytelling structures, the development of characterisation and much more.

The nature of qualitative audience research is that it reveals what Schoenmakers terms 'reception results', rather than allowing us to examine 'reception processes' (1990). That is, in this case, it uncovers what children make of the performance after the event, rather than the precise cognitive processes by which the children decoded the performance as they watched it. It is possible, however, to explore this question through the children's own consciousness of the process, and it is particularly striking that many of the children not only had the ability to read the stage but also possessed a conscious awareness of the conventions of staging. They could, when prompted and directed by questioning and the drawing process, describe *how* they knew what they knew about the performance.

So, for example, Eleanor (figure 6.1) drew a fully realised depiction of one moment of the story from *Them With Tails*. In her drawing we can see a Princess's bedroom, a Badger and a King.

Figure 6.1: The Princess, the King and the Badger by Eleanor

We asked Eleanor about this drawing and the moment depicted. How did she know what to draw? For example:

> **Researcher**: How did you know she had a pink dress?
>
> **Eleanor**: Because at the back there was a pink thing ... at the back showing that it was a pink dress.

Eleanor is accurately describing the theatrical convention used by the performers in *Them With Tails:* to illustrate the various characters they adopted, they wore different hats or clipped different tails onto their belts. So the Jackal had a grey furry tail and the Princess a few strips of pink cloth. These signified and pointed towards the missing whole, a semiotic shorthand that the children could comprehend. What is more, they could follow the signification of the tails within the context of a wider system of characterisation that utilised gestures, body language and voice in a manner that did not always adhere to the actual tail being worn. So, for example, the performer playing the Princess might suddenly switch and play her father, the King, still wearing the pink tail, but now signified differently through voice or body language. Significantly, Eleanor drew three characters when in fact there were only ever two performers on the stage. This again is an indication of the children's theatrical literacy, their ability to understand which theatrical signs to pay attention to at particular moments and which to ignore.

At other times the different signifying elements cohered, and the children were able to recognise this too:

Faiqa: The person that played the princess was a man.

Researcher: Ok. How was that looking, a man playing the princess?

Faiqa: It was quite girly voice.

Researcher: He put on a girly voice. What else did he do?

Faiqa: He had this tiny little piece of a dress on at the back of his legs. That's what made him a princess.

Like Eleanor, Faiqa is able to accurately isolate and identify the various signs that communicated to her that the male performer was playing a female character – and, as this exchange illustrates, she could not only follow such conventions but verbalise them.

In the research, two school classes watched *Them With Tails*: a group of seven to eight year olds and a younger set of five to six year olds. Unsurprisingly, this ability consciously to reflect back upon how they were able to interpret the production was more noticeable among the older children. However, the younger children not only showed strong competence at reading the stage, as demonstrated clearly in their drawings and by their behaviour during the performance, but at times they could also consciously reflect back on this process, as in this exchange with a six year old:

Researcher: Was it a real chicken? [Angel shakes head] What was it?

Angel: It was a pretend chicken. He put a thing on his head to make a chicken.

Researcher: To make a chicken. What else did he do to make himself like a chicken?

Angel: He put feathers on.

Researcher: Feathers, right. Was there anything that he did to make himself be like a chicken?

Angel: He went... [flaps arms, makes chicken noise].

Here Angel demonstrates her theatrical competence in two ways: firstly through verbal reflective deduction; secondly through mimicry. It is worth noting here that the children often used mimicry, gesture, movement and other non-linguistic actions to communicate knowledge about the production. Through this it was apparent that the children often knew things, and knew that they knew them, but did not have the vocabulary through which to express them – or alternatively simply felt that non-verbal forms of communication were more appropriate.

As well as such bodily knowledge, the children also exhibited other kinds of engagement with the production. For example, as already mentioned, they readily internalised the key theatrical convention in the production by which a tail stood in for the entire character or creature. In one instance this process of interpretation was particularly striking, although far from typical, when James began the workshop by starting to draw a wolf's tail:

> **Researcher**: How did you know it was a wolf?
>
> **James**: Cos it had the colour of the wolf's tail. Cos the wolf's tail are the same colour as that [pointing to his drawing].

Entirely unprompted, James then asked for a pair of scissors and cut out his picture in order to produce something he could put on, making himself a tail just like the ones seen in the production. James spent most of the rest of the workshop perfecting his wolf tail – and a second one to take home for his little brother – and asking for help in how to attach it to his trousers.

What James demonstrates here is a practical knowledge of what all the children had read from the production – that the tail costumes stood in for a whole character; that a wolf tail meant a whole wolf.

Interpreting the stage

Many of the same observations about the children's broad theatrical competence, and awareness of this theatrical literacy, can be made about responses to *Martha*. The production was very different from *Them With Tails*: The narrative and staging was much more complete, more about showing the children, less about working with their imagination. Nonetheless, as theatre there were gaps in the staging, such as the puppet goose as previously discussed, where the children had to engage and work in order for the production to be meaningful to them. The children's drawings largely completed these gaps, in some instances producing pictures that were entirely based around depicting things evoked referentially but not presented on stage.

Again, we can detect in the children's conversations a self-awareness about how they interpreted the production:

> **Researcher**: And the sun is shining. How did you know it was a nice day?

Robbie: Well, I heard noises so I thought it was like a nice day.

Researcher: What kind of noises?

Robbie: Sort of seagulls and I heard a wee bit of sun. Because I hear some things a lot.

Robbie's evocation of synaesthesia here – 'I heard a wee bit of sun' – may be unusually poetical, but it is also completely accurate. Robbie saw the performance in the school hall, and therefore without any lighting effects. Perception of the sun was produced primarily through auditory clues – sound effects of sunny-day-ness such as seagulls or people having fun on the beach – or embedded references such as one character saying to another 'nice day isn't it?' These were supported by other visual signs – such as the hanging up of washing or characters wearing shorts or sunglasses – that together built a comprehensive idea of sunshine. These clues were translated into the visual medium of the children's drawings in the form of the conventionalised representation of a sunny day. Importantly, however, they were then able to articulate why they had drawn the sunny day representation.

This is an example not only of the children's theatrical literacy – their ability to read and interpret various kinds of theatrical signs and turn this mentally into a fully fledged representation – but additionally indicates a conscious awareness of such signs and the ability to describe how they knew what they knew about the performance.

Another example is apparent in one girl's response to being asked about the details she had drawn in her picture of Martha and her house. All the children had noticed these small details – including things such as an Irn-Bru can with two straws, a half eaten piece of toast, a pair of snorkelling flippers, various bits of beach debris and many more. Jodi's drawing reproduced many of these:

Researcher: That is quite a lot of detail to notice, were there lots of little details in the play?

Jodi: Aha.

Researcher: Why were they important?

Jodi: To show you what kind of lifestyle she was living in.

Her answer is entirely accurate and this kind of observation linking detail to meaning was fairly typical. Two boys, for example, became involved in a complex discussion over the geographic location for the play, trying to reconcile the otherwise clearly Scottish setting, which they identified through

Martha's accent, vocabulary and other references, with the conflicting signification of the postman's American accent and the American style post-box.

Individually such connections are relatively minor, but collectively they illustrate the ability of not just being able to understand the theatrical presentation, but also to reflect upon that understanding. With *Martha* this could also be seen in the children's ability to reflect upon the operation of the goose puppet and appreciate it both in terms of the evoked experience and the technique.

Not getting the performance

This analysis could be continued into the third production seen by children participating in this research: the puppet show *Psst!* That the majority of children were able to produce meaningful pictures of the performance indicates that they possessed the competence required to engage with and 'get' the production. As we have seen, their discussion of the workings of the puppets also indicated a dual level of awareness, between the material and the evoked experience. More interesting, however, is that there were aspects of the children's responses to *Psst!* suggesting that they did not fully engage with the performance.

One indication of this was the way the children focused in their drawings and conversations on the puppets as characters operating in a largely abstracted universe, downgrading any narrative elements of the production and largely neglecting the evoked world of the circus. While in their conversations the children clearly indicated that they knew the production was set around some kind of circus, they were largely uninterested in talking about this.

This lack of interest could be taken as an instance of a wider lack of communality between the children and *Psst!* as a production. It is difficult to identify this perception, but it is apparent in what the children largely did not do in this instance that other children did in response to the other productions. So not only did the children not represent the referential world of the circus, they did not engage in retelling the story to the same extent they had with the other productions. While pictures in response to *Martha* and *Them With Tails* present a fairly even mix between depicting a character in isolation and one within a setting, those in response to *Psst!* overwhelming depict characters in isolation and extremely rarely against an evoked setting. Additionally, while the drawings of other productions are mostly of specific moments, identifiable scenes or stories, those of *Psst!* are largely abstracted and non-particular – they are just of the figures.

The responses to *Psst!* are interesting. They are clearly not the result of any inability to read the theatrical presentation. Other aspects of their drawings and conversation indicate that the children in this instance have the same levels of theatrical competence as the children from the other groups. They are exhibiting particular problems with this particular production.

No production is perfect, and one reason the children were not working with *Psst!* in a manner that developed the illusion and narrative was probably because it was not working for them. Perhaps this was the case with elements of the performance and the quality of the piece itself. More subtly, however, *Psst!* was radically different in terms of its production style from most performances that its Scottish audiences would have seen. As programmer of the Imaginate Festival, Tony Reekie says that he booked the piece because he felt there was a real quality in the performance, but he was aware that it was potentially risky:

> It was about the mood as much as anything else, about the creation of the world, about the manipulation of the puppets, it was about that concept of the little running gag that was going through it.... It had threads going through it, which were nice in terms of being quite different for an audience which is just used to people shouting at them, who are really just used to that... so it was always going to be a slight risk... There was almost like a sense, 'when does this start'... It was a different kind of experience for them. (personal interview, 2007)

Reekie also candidly observes that while the production had always seemed to be working very well on the occasions he saw it in Europe, in front of a Scottish audience it 'wasn't as successful as I thought it was going to be in terms of reception.'

The possible reasons for this are subtle and multiple, perhaps to do with generally different levels of children's theatrical experience between Scotland and Europe. The subtlety of the production, dependent on producing a quiet and focused atmosphere that evoked a particular world of the circus and operated through small details and the very precise manipulation of the puppets, meant that it was particularly exposed to disruption or to lack of attention. In terms of its reception during the several performances I watched, *Psst!* did not fail its Scottish audience in that it was not enjoyed, nor did the audience fail the production in refusing to engage and work with it. But it is fair to say that the young audience did not have all the tools or experience to deal with the stark difference in its theatrical tone and abstract, elusive nature.

As Jeanne Klein points out, when watching theatre 'children will attend to that content they expect to understand and will work to understand it, especially if the information interests them personally' (2005:47). Here they responded by focusing on those elements that meant something to them. In contrast, other aspects of the production were largely ignored which, Klein suggests, is often the case with material perceived as 'too novel, complex, surprising'.

The young Scottish audience responded to *Psst!* on an immediate level. Perhaps their responses indicate something about the position of the theatre experience within our culture and within our schools, where entertainment and the immediate response predominate. The limits of theatrical competence, therefore, are marked by limits of experience and of expectation, and also perhaps on having the tools as spectators to deal with performances in the manner required here. Within the limitations of their response, there is the opportunity to think about what more might be possible, about how responses can not only be extended, but also made more subtle and reflective in manner. The question would be what processes could be provided that would engage our young audiences to get the most out of all productions; these are developed further in Part Three of this book.

A question of venue

When talking to people working in the theatre industry about this research, they often ask me whether my findings could reflect on the importance of the venue to children's responses to theatre. They want to know whether audiences respond differently to performances seen in formal theatre spaces as compared with those seen in a school hall.

There are a whole set of interests behind this question, relating to the practicalities of delivering theatre to young children and the relative costs and disturbances of taking children to the theatre or taking a production to a school. But the question is really about all sorts of other things: atmosphere, expectations and the social experience of going to the theatre. From the perspective of those working in the theatre industry, the production in a school hall is demonstrably a different kind of experience from that in the theatre. In terms of audience development, of introducing children to theatre and perhaps instilling in them a life-long interest and habitus, the trip to the theatre is perceived as being much more valuable. In some sense, what children see in the school hall may be a performance, but it is not theatre as a cultural entity. This perception was echoed by some of the participants in this research, as in the following exchange:

Researcher: Does sometimes your school get turned into a theatre?

Kristofer: No.

Researcher: Do you ever have anybody coming in doing plays in the hall?

Kristofer: See these silver bits and things? [pointing to a stack of stage risers in the corner]

Researcher: Mmmm.

Kristofer: They're the stage, cos the stage gets set up in here.

Researcher: So because there's a stage in here, does that make it a theatre?

Kristofer: It does look like a theatre except it isn't.

Researcher: But what is it then?

Kristofer: It's just a play.

For Kristofer, theatre is the building, the atmosphere, the audience, the occasion; productions in the school hall are just plays. Anthony Clark asserts that staging productions in schools 'has the effect, unfortunately, of marginalising the work within the profession, and limiting a child's experience of the full potential of this collaborative medium' (2002:28).

This was not a question that this project specifically set out to investigate and, although the research included performances both in formal venues and school halls, the number of variables means it is difficult to come to a firm conclusion. However, in a chapter on theatrical competences, I would like to make this point.

Them With Tails was seen by two different schools. One group went to see it at the Traverse Theatre in Edinburgh, while the other watched it in their school hall. On both occasions the production involved several scenes where the audience were asked to shout out suggestions for the actors: the children were invited to name the central character, to provide a special power, to suggest where something was happening or what, the rampaging clay pot boy ate next. When this occurred at the Traverse, suggestions were made enthusiastically with the result that the clay pot boy ate: barrels of sweets, one thousand pandas, his mother and father and a small boy called Simon. These suggestions originated across the whole audience. I know these were the suggestions because the children remembered them, repeated them and often drew them. India's drawing (figure 6.2) represents another participative moment in the Traverse Theatre performance, accurately depicting how the audience's suggestions caused another story to include a pink castle and a fat sumo wrestler named Bob (figure 9.4).

Figure 6.2: The audience by India

In contrast, the suggestions made during the school hall performance are hazier in my memory and were infrequently included in the children's drawings, but I think in this performance the clay pot boy ate grapes, bread and chocolate. These suggestions came from the children, but they did not seem to remember them or depict them in their drawings. It is fairly clear then that the suggestions made in the Traverse performance were better, in that they were funnier, fitted the absurdity of the story, provided appropriate challenges for the performers and were more memorable. The children participating in the research appreciated them for all these reasons.

This suggests that the experience of being in a large, mixed audience was a learning experience, providing models of participatory behaviour the children could enjoy and adopt. Take for example the children's enjoyment of a suggestion that they did not fully understand, when somebody in the audience suggested that a mermaid be called Rambo. During the performance, the actors incorporated various connotations linked to this name into the action and these aspects were remembered, repeated and mimicked by the children in the workshops. But they did not have a clue who or what Rambo was. Instead, part of their appreciation was that of younger children gaining an insight into the knowledge possessed by those older than them. In contrast, the school hall audience, which included a single year group, was more homogenous and had no alternative models to follow. Although there are clear challenges for any production playing to a broad audience, for young spectators being in a heterogeneous audience can provide opportunities for learning.

Theatrical competence

We quite often asked the children 'how did you know...?' How did you know the princess had a long nose? How did you know it was a sunny day? Essentially we were asking the children to think about what the production used to communicate to them – set, lighting, costumes, music and so on. The children could usually answer sensibly and accurately, indicating in effect, the beginnings of a semiotic analysis linking theatrical 'signs' to their meaning.

Overall, the children's responses, both in drawing and conversation, indicated that they possessed a strong theatrical competence. The children had internalised an understanding of what theatre is – people on stage pretending to be or do things. They had the ability to 'get' a performance and to swiftly recognise and decode different theatrical techniques. This is, I suggest, a cultural ability that is largely taken for granted – a semiotic ability that often develops passively as children grow and learn the languages of dramatic representation at the same time as they learn speech. Klein, drawing on her own research, affirms this observation when she remarks that by the age of six, children have

> already constructed basic story schemas for drama, having role-played their own scripts in pretend play since the age of three; and they know many theatrical conventions from watching television and film. (2005:44)

Although often taken for granted, this cultural competence is a fairly advanced skill and should be recognised.

Additionally, while typically lacking the vocabulary through which to articulate their knowledge easily, not only could the children decode the stage performances but they could also analyse and reflect upon their decoding. The degree to which this was the case varied according to age, but also to other factors, including their theatre-going experience and the confidence and comfort they exhibited in drawing and visual representation. Crucially, there was pleasure in the exercising of this ability to read and analyse the workings of the performance. Their consciousness of the theatrical processes, and appreciation of those processes enhanced the children's ability and willingness to engage with the theatrical experience. The pleasure in analysing the theatrical presentation is the pleasure of competence – that is, of understanding – and also the pleasure of knowledge: of gaining insights and specialist knowledge.

There are two lessons from this. Firstly, there is no need to worry about children's ability to comprehend a stage performance. Even for those who have little theatrical experience, the skills are there to be able to read the stage. Certainly, greater experience provides greater competence and greater self-reflective ability, and this enhances the experience. However, the theatrical experiences we offer children need not be simple ones.

Secondly, we do not need to worry about a performance filling in all the gaps and can on the whole assume that children will work with a production, engaging with it on their own terms and with their own imagination. We can see a positive benefit from the amount of space *Them With Tails* provided for the audience to engage with and complete the performance. The pleasure for the audience was in this imaginative engagement, in being able to see what was being done and rise to the challenge of responding in kind.

However, some of the responses to *Psst!* remind us of the two-way relationship between theatre and its audiences. The audience have to be able and willing to work with the production, which in turn has to work with and for its audience. *Psst!* was not a bad performance, as evidenced by the fact that its audience enjoyed it. Except in certain specific ways, however, the children did not then take this experience and develop it further through their imagination, interpretation or emotional engagement. The ability to establish enduring resonances and meanings for its audience can be seen as a particular marker of quality in art form experiences, and the possible forms of such extended engagement is the subject of later chapters.

The limited responses to *Psst!* also remind us that we should not necessarily rely on children's passively developed cultural competences but should look for ways of pro-actively extending their abilities, particularly to reflect critically and consciously upon and evaluate their experiences. It is important to recognise that theatrical pleasure for young children is intellectual and reflective, as well as located within immediate enjoyment. This suggests that children gain pleasure from the task of looking and interpreting, that they appreciate the challenge and the involvement of their own skills of spectatorship and that, if encouraged, they will engage in looking again and looking longer.

7

Moral or Metaphorical Engagement

Many professionals and teachers consider the potential for theatre to have a social or moral effect on young audiences a major benefit of engagement with the art form. The belief is that the moral or social messages of a production can have a direct positive impact on children's minds and their relationship with the world. As Peter Brosius writes, theatre for young people is often engaged in 'addressing critical issues in young people's lives' in the hope that this will inform and empower the audience (2001:75).

Danish children's theatre producer Peter Manscher makes similar comments when he declares that 'No subject should be too dangerous for an audience of children. But the way we handle delicate or difficult subjects has to be chosen with care, respect and solidarity with the child.' Manscher continues with the following anecdote:

> In the early 90s the theatre Artibus produced a quite famous show entitled *The 4th Commandment* ('Thou shalt respect thy father and thy mother') about child abuse. The play dealt with a child who grows up in an atmosphere of violence – in the borderland between upbringing and abuse. One of the child's lines is: 'How can he think that I will stop crying, while he's beating me up and it hurts?' The audience witnessed the child in a series of moving and grotesque scenes that were very realistic and even frightening. There was not even a happy ending in the play, and many adults commented that this was much too tough on the children. But Artibus experienced after nearly every show that at least one young spectator came up and thanked them for showing that she was not alone with her worries and fears.

For Manscher, theatre provides an opportunity for 'social dialogue and under-standing between children and adults'; a space somewhere outside of others, such as education or parenting, where a different kind of conversation can take place. Brian McMaster's articulation of excellence, introduced in Chapter Three, is also worth returning to here, as he writes about how the arts can

> help us make sense of our place in the world, ask questions we would not otherwise have asked, understand the answers in ways we couldn't otherwise have understood and appreciate things we have never before experienced. (2008:9)

Jeanne Klein, although arguing that such perceptions of empowering impacts are somewhat romanticised, asserts that 'the hallmark of aesthetic experience lies in spectators' recognition and articulation of metaphoric and moral applications of a play's themes to self and society' (2005:50). Such perceptions suggest that the primary objective of watching a performance can be reduced to one of decoding of meaning in the form of thematic content and empathetic response. Indeed, Klein writes in one paper about children's 'failure to make spontaneous metaphoric connections from the fiction world' of the performance to their own personal lives and the world at large (1989:12). While such responses are significant, to give them such primacy – indicated by the word *failure* – is an overly narrow perception. It neglects the importance of other kinds of responses, such as in terms of spectacle and play, or the possibility that some element of the theatrical form itself may be the principal meaning of the performance. It also seems to attribute value to only plays that convey moral or metaphoric associations and this, as shall be seen, causes particular problems for some of the productions seen by the children featured in this book.

Of the productions seen in connection with this research, it is only with *Martha* that response focused on a moral or social application could be expected. So, it is the children's responses to the explicitly moral content of *Martha* that are now examined.

Friendship

For an adult audience, Catherine Wheels' production has a fairly explicit moral. The play begins with Martha as a miserable old bissum, refusing the offers of friendship from the postman, hoisting a flag over her house that says 'go away' and trying to shoo off the goose. The narrative then follows how Martha's grudging acceptance of the goose's presence transforms into genuine affection that allows her to be both sad and understanding when the goose leaves to rejoin his family. At the end of the play, Martha is shown accepting the postman's invitation of friendship.

For young children, friendship is clearly of immediate concern and the play's message about the importance of friends was echoed by many of the workshop participants. They communicated this by illustrating a smiling Martha going off with the postman at the end of the production or explaining that they have drawn her smiling because of her friendship with the goose:

Researcher: What do you think Martha was feeling that you've drawn? She looks like she's got a little smile.

Helena: Cos she's happy she's brought the goose in because she starts to make friends with it.

Researcher: And that's made her happy, has it?

Helena: Because she used to be a bossy person but as soon as the goose came round she started being nice and everything.

Researcher: So has the goose changed her then?

Helena: The goose has changed her. I think the goose has just been playing tricks on her to say like, just to get her to be a nice person and everything.

Similarly Ronan asserted that this change in Martha was the most important thing in the production:

Researcher: What do you think you'll remember most about the play?

Ronan: I think I'll remember that she was all like, she wasn't very nice at the start and she became, she became a friendly person.

Thus in this sense the children perceived and decoded the meaning of the production. Klein, however, offers important cautions to such a straightforward assertion when she notes that the majority of children interpret thematic concepts within plays, such as friendship, 'simply by recounting what characters said and did within performance' (2005:51). This seems to be borne out by these responses, which present the meaning of friendship in terms of the events undergone by Martha in a way that constructs the experiences as occurring at a distance. Although we could argue that the fact that the children recount these themes marks their importance to them, Klein rightly observes that they are retold in a way that 'may appear to have no relevant bearing on their personal lives' (2005:51).

One noticeable exception to this in this production was Karen's discussion of her picture of the scene where the goose leaves Martha (figure 7.1):

Researcher: Why is the goose crying?

Karen: Because it is sad to leave, but it is also happy.

Figure 7.1: The goose crying by Karen

Researcher: That's a complicated emotion [Karen: Yeah]. So why is he sad and why is he happy?

Karen: Because he's happy that he's going, and he's sad that he is leaving a friend.

Researcher: Yes, do you think there is a lesson there, or an important message?

Karen: Yeah.

Researcher: Yes, what's that?

Karen: It's that, he really really like... he tried to make her think of being friendly to other people.

Researcher: Do you think it's important that the play had a message?

Karen: Yeah.... Because, because it might help my brother and get some more friends. Because, because he's being bullied at the moment.

Karen has clearly abstracted the thematic content of the production and applied it to an experience within her own life. Perhaps Karen's response, however, also illustrates another aspect of Klein's argument, which is that:

Plays [are] more likely [to] affirm and reinforce conceptual ideas already learned than 'teach' youngsters 'new' information that they don't already know and recognize. In other words, a child may abstract metaphoric applications because she already knows and has experienced the same analogous situation in her life. (2005:51)

This description certainly matches Karen's position, and leads Klein to pose a conundrum: if we produce plays which present children with new thematic lessons, they are unlikely to be able to universalise them or apply them meaningfully to their own; whereas if we present them with plays 'in which children can (already) enter into protagonists' realities, we are simply replicating their current experiential knowledge. This factor then explains another reason for their restless, impatient behaviors during performances – been there, done that' (2005:51). Elsewhere Klein notes that 'theatre does not appear to alter children's attitudes about human situations; rather, it reinforces and confirms what they already know through experience as 'truth'' (1993:16).

The nature of the productions seen meant that my research did not focus on this element directly and therefore cannot address the first aspect of the conundrum regarding children's ability to learn from previously unknown thematic content. However, Klein does seem significantly to undervalue the importance for children of seeing their own experiences and knowledge enacted and represented. Far from simply replicating current experiential knowledge, this replication plays a part in affirming children's perceptions and supporting their own judgements. Martin Drury, for example, describes how the arts provide a powerful and 'distinctive way for children to make meaning, to make sense of their selves and of the world' (2006:151). This certainly seems to be the case for Karen, for whom *Martha* was a useful affirmation of her own experience. Far from showing restlessness because of the known quality of the production, the engaged nature of Karen's drawings and conversations suggests the opposite: the production had particular meaning for her precisely *because* it affirmed her experiential knowledge.

The other two productions connected to this project are more problematic since they cannot be easily considered in terms of their moral or thematic content. It would be difficult for anybody to construct a moral or metaphoric reading of *Psst!* and the children certainly did not respond to the performance in that manner. The closest comment came from Bailey when she said the performance 'was about being quiet'. With *Them With Tails* the situation is more complicated. Some of the tales, which drew on folkloric or fable-like traditions, did contain moral lessons about greed, deceitfulness or ambition.

The children, however, almost entirely ignored these, observation on such themes arising only on the rare occasions when they were explicitly asked whether there had been a moral to the stories. The responses were brief and interestingly literal, as in this instance:

> **Researcher**: Do you think there was a moral to that story, a lesson that you should learn?
>
> **Aiman**: Yes.
>
> **Researcher**: What was the lesson?
>
> **Aiman**: Don't eat other people's things.
>
> **Researcher**: Did the other stories have a lesson, a moral?
>
> **Aiman**: The, erm, the one of them was to not make a clay pot boy.

To an extent this affirms Klein's perception that children will often simply recount the events of the narrative rather than draw out a personal or universal lesson. In this case, such a lesson might have been about greed or playing god, but instead becomes comical. However, from this material it is much more significant that the children's attention was elsewhere – on the narrative, the humour, the spectacle and the formal style – which in the context of this particular production was entirely appropriate. We might often presume that it is with a moral lesson or thematic content that a production's main idea or meaning can be located, particularly in theatre for children which has traditionally had fairly didactic purposes. However, the meaning of *Them With Tails* lay in the nature of the performance itself. Similarly, if called upon to identify the main idea of *Psst!* it would be, as Bailey identified, best located in the atmosphere created and the manner in which the puppets were manipulated.

With *Martha*, most of the children would probably have been able to identify the central idea of the play as being about friendship. In contrast to Klein, I would argue that the representation of such known themes has an important role to play in enacting and reaffirming children's own knowledge and sense of the world. However, I would assert that what the children learnt from *Martha* deviated widely from this theme, their attention being focused on the nature of the theatrical presentation and the communication of the illusion.

Although the image of the crying goose predominates in Karen's drawing, we also consider its presentation of other elements of her experience. This includes a very complete imaginative transformation of puppet into real goose and the striking use of perspective so that the picture is visualised from high in the air. It seems to be both condescending and dictatorial to perceive theatre for young people as being primarily about the communication of moral lessons. Instead, and much more broadly, theatre provides models of ways in which the world can be understood.

Part Three
Enhancing Engagement

8
Enhancing Engagement

Earlier I explored questions of quality and ambition in theatre for children, and asked how we assess such subjective criteria and what we hope young audiences will gain from their theatrical encounters. I suggested that one way of thinking about quality is in terms of the ability of a work of art to make us consider it and the world harder, for longer and in more detail. Quality in a cultural experience is its enduring resonance as it engages us intellectually, imaginatively or emotionally. This is certainly the case with theatre that is made for adults and we should have the same ambition for theatre made for children.

A piece of theatre for children typically lasts no longer than 60 minutes. After that it is over. Often those 60 minutes are viewed as a self-contained entity, separated from the rest of the child's life. There is nothing inherently wrong with this. If the audience are entertained for those 60 minutes, that is fabulous. But perhaps we should ask for this and more. One criterion of quality in theatre for children, as for adult theatre, is the ability to provide pleasure in the moment of the experience, *and* pleasure in an enduring, extended engagement.

This interest in the extended encounter is a feature of philosophical conceptualisations of what it means to experience art. These place emphasis on not only the immediate sensory engagement but also on what the individual does reflectively with and through that engagement. As Clive Cazeaux puts it, in elaboration of Immanual Kant's ideas on aesthetic engagement: 'experience is not the reception of sense impressions but a form of prospection or questioning. To have an experience is to be in an active state of finding out about the world' (2000:67).

In *Art and Experience,* John Dewey similarly asserts that although 'on common conception, the work of art is often identified with the building, book, painting [etc], the actual work of art is what the product does with and in experience' (1934:3). With theatre, therefore, what is important is not just what happens on the stage but also what happens within the minds, imagination and memory of the watching audience. Such perceptions of the nature of aesthetic experience are not written in the specific context of young audiences, but I see no reason why our aspirations for children and young people's artistic engagement should be any different than they are for adults.

We have seen that children have the competences and skills to understand complex theatrical performances and engage with them on a number of levels. At the same time, however, unless children are invited or actively encouraged to take that engagement further it exists primarily on an immediate level. That is, it lasts the 60 minutes of the performance.

We could legitimately argue that this is fair enough. But that would neglect the richness and playfulness of the responses that emerged when children *do* take the narratives or characters or techniques forward for themselves. It would also be to neglect how such increased engagement marks a deepening and extending of the children's knowledge and ownership – creative, imaginative, emotional and technical – of the performance.

Experience plus

In her discussion of young children's aesthetic engagement with theatre, Jeanne Klein constructs two broad categories of spectator attention. The first is the 'ritualistic viewer', who watches for entertainment or escapism, in a largely passive manner and with little mental effort. The second is the 'instrumental viewer', who actively seeks out social information from a production, investing high mental effort and looking to integrate new messages into their existing knowledge (2005:44-6). Klein suggests that a range of factors can influence the type of use to which children put a performance, such as the school setting, pupil's own choices, emotional mood and the teacher's framing of the event.

Within the school context this last point is clearly vital, and one justification of theatre for children rests upon its educational and therefore instrumental impact. Theatre companies, artists and education workers have increasingly co-operated in the production and utilisation of teachers' packs and other resources supporting a performance. These packs typically suggest activities designed to facilitate exploration of the themes and characters presented in the production and frequently construct links with key aspects of children's development and learning.

There is no evidence or clear evaluation of the effectiveness of such resource packs. The quality of some of the work resulting from children's engagement with theatre through these packs is no doubt high, but the extent to which they are adopted and their real benefits or impacts are unknown. However, as discussed in Chapter One, some commentators have expressed concerns that the focus on fitting into curricula requirements can damage the excellence of the production and the theatrical experience itself. Lyn Gardner, for example, observes that 'I see too many shows whose driving force is clearly not a passion to make theatre, but a passion to sell a product whose major selling point is the way it ties in with the National Curriculum' (2002:35). My own perception is that the specificity of some production resource packs and the way they are tailored to particular productions and designed to bring out particular themes is a limiting factor – they can make watching resemble a decoding exercise of spotting themes and responding accordingly. Anecdotally, I find that such resources tend to flatten and homogenise the experiences and responses produced.

It is also worth thinking about how the implicit purpose of teacher's packs and other resources is to transform ritualistic viewers into instrumental spectators. And while the transformation of a passive, ritualistic audience into a thinking one sounds attractive at first, it might also present some concerns.

Klein herself warns against this, suggesting that pre-performance learning has the potential to remove all surprises from the production and result in the experience becoming 'a comparative exercise of previously learned information' (2005:46). In a personal note she continues:

> Although I provide teachers with study guides for every production as they've come to expect, I actually hate them, because I personally want theatre to astonish me. [...] Instead, I believe all understanding should come from the production itself and not from a study guide. (2005:56)

On an artistic principle Klein is surely right. But as a way of introducing, engaging and educating audiences this is an overly purist attitude. It fails to recognise that for some children and young people, as explored in Chapter Two, lack of required cultural capital and habitus can actively exclude them from arts engagement in a manner that simple exposure to an art work cannot resolve on its own.

This debate makes interesting connections with the discussion in Part One about quality in children's theatre and the relationship between early years arts experiences and future theatre-going habits. I suggested that quality is related to the ambition for richer and more involved engagement in theatre performance. Resources packs and other conscious efforts to enhance children's engagement run the risk of educationalising the experience. However, we do need critically to assess the nature of children's engagement with theatre and simple exposure to performance might have limited impact. It seems reasonable that children's experience of theatre should be facilitated to invite them to engage with the performance in an active, self-reflective and empowered manner, which extends the imaginative and intellectual afterlife of their experiences.

Memory, reflection and transformation

Sarah: I need to start off remembering.

Researcher: Yeah, that's a good idea. Let's start of by thinking about what you're going to draw. What do you remember?

Sarah: I remember the sun.

Researcher: What was the sun in? Was there a sun in a story?

Sarah: No, it was outside.

Researcher: Was it in any of the stories, the sun?

Sarah: Ah, I remember.

A defining feature of theatre and live performance is that it is not there when you come to talk about it afterwards. Unlike visual art, videos, novels or stories, we are unable to control the speed at which we watch a live performance, cannot re-play, re-read or re-watch and cannot re-consult it after the event. The ephemerality of theatre gives the experience a particular character, which is marked by the fleeting passage of the performance – if you miss something you cannot retrieve it – and makes demands of memory after the event. As Peter Brook puts it, theatre 'is an event for that moment in time, for that audience in that place – and it's gone. Gone without a trace' (cited in Melzer, 1995:148).

In my research I asked children to remember the performance they had seen and to engage in a process that included factual retrieval and imaginative reconstruction. Some of them had seen it that morning, others the day before. In all cases it was no longer there. The play was gone, all that was left were their memories – or lack of them:

Robyn: I don't know, because I can't remember.

Researcher: You can't remember anything?

Robyn: Mmmmmm.

Researcher: I'm sure you can.

Robyn: No, I can't.

When reading transcripts that demonstrated the children's working through of memory, one should recognise that saying 'I can't remember', 'I don't know' or 'I can't think of anything' were devices they used to evade having to think about or answer our questions. Often it was an unthinking reflex, perhaps a way of not having to commit or expose themselves. In most instances it allowed the children space and time to think and respond in their own way. We found that a useful way of overcoming this response was playfully acknowledging the reason they were saying 'I don't know':

Researcher: Oh, Michael, your pictures look really good now. Now you were brave to start. What have you drawn for us? Who's this?

Michael: I don't know.

Researcher [laughing]: You do know. You just don't want to tell me.

Of course 'I can't remember' could also be genuine and was sometimes said with frustration:

Chantelle: I remember what happened to the boy.

Researcher: What happened to the boy?

Chantelle: Yeah...when the, oh, what was it, I've forgotten again.

The objective of the post-performance research workshops was not to test the children on the accuracy or extent of their memory of the performance. This is in direct contrast to the work of Jeanne Klein who in one piece of research sets out to test children's recall through their ability to place photographic images of a performance in sequence (1989:10). We had noticed during an initial pilot workshop that our questioning had a tendency towards memory testing and sought to move away from this to embrace more playful and transformative possibilities. Consequently our research did not set out to measure or assess the children's recall abilities and we could not tell how well the children remembered the performance when they joined us for the workshops. What is clear, however, is that by the end of the sessions they remembered, or consciously recalled, a lot more than they had at the beginning:

Researcher: So what happened to make things end happily?

Ben: Can't remember.

Researcher: You can't remember. Well maybe if you carry on drawing you might start to remember more when you draw the bird.

Ben: I remember now.

Researcher: You remember now, what happened?

Ben: I'll remember it ever and ever... I'll remember it ever and ever...

Engaging their memories of the production through conversation and drawing required the children to remember more about what they had seen than if they had been left alone. Although at times they responded by declaring that they could not remember anything, the research process provided them with structures through which to develop their memories and with active and interested listeners with whom they could share their experiences and interpretations. This encouraged the children to value their own perspectives and to think about what they had seen, to make connections and begin to formulate opinions.

The evidence for this is difficult to isolate and extract because it does not occur in specific instances or exchanges but in the minutiae of observations, remarks, newly re-established connections and in the drawings themselves. We see it in the way the four exchanges quoted above moved rapidly on afterwards into a moment of satisfactory and rewarding recollection, expressed verbally or in a drawing. This is a fairly common-sense observation – if you spend any time reflecting on something, you begin consciously to remember more about it – but is still worth pointing out. For one thing, these observations contain the implicit suggestion that unless the children are actively encouraged to remember, and to develop and reflect on their memories, they do not. For another, it assists our thinking about what strategies help young audiences most effectively. And finally, there is the evident enjoyment and benefit that facilitated recollection brought to the children.

Also worth stressing is that these memories involved both acts of factual recall and imaginative reconstruction. Human memory is fallible; it is subject to forgetfulness and transformation. In certain circumstances where accurate, factual recall is the goal, the transformative character of children's memory is problematic. Within theatre, however, there exists a tradition asserting that the memory of a performance should be valued in terms not of accurate recall but of transformative reconstruction. For example, Eugenio Barba argues that the meaning of a performance is not what was happening on stage but what is happening in the minds and subsequently the memories of the audience:

> In the age of electronic memory, of films, and of reproducibility, theatre performance also defines itself through the work that living memory, which is not museum but metamorphosis, is obliged to do. (1992:78)

Clearly, Barba does not value audience memory *despite* its imperfect metamorphosis of what really happened, but *because* of it. Memory, he argues, is in this transformative, multiple and mobile nature closer to the essential identity of live theatre after, not before, it has undergone such transformations. Taking such perspectives on board, we need to consider children's continuing engagement with performances in terms of deepening their factual memory and understanding through reflection and analysis and through their transformative engagement within creative play. Most significant and creative are those moments when these elements coincide and new insights and responses emerge.

Rather than the specific, narrowing and sometimes closed nature of theatre resource packs, it is this kind of active, open and self-reflective engagement that the ideas and methodologies presented in the following two chapters seek to elicit. Their purpose is not just to stimulate factual recall or test memory but to develop reflection, play, transformation and knowledge. The chapters explore what kinds of afterlife a performance has in a child's memory, consider how this afterlife might be extended and ask questions about how children actively play with their experiences – particularly through drawing and conversation. The chapters are focused around the understanding that engaging children with theatre involves more than sitting them down in front of a production – more than simple exposure to the arts. It involves a responsibility to contextualise, enhance and frame the experience.

These chapters are aimed particularly at artists, researchers, students and teachers who need to engage young children in dialogue about their artistic and theatre experiences. They are intended as toolboxes to help guide the deepening of children's experiences. Accordingly, they seek to conflate the positions of artist, teacher and researcher, seeing all as engaged in aesthetic enquiry with children.

9

Drawing on the Experience

Drawing is used to enable children to think, feel and communicate in a variety of contexts. In art therapy for example, children's art works have long been used as a reflective and mediating tool through which to explore and uncover experience, feeling and memory. Kate Pahl suggests that drawing helps children to externalise thought (cited in Coates, 2004:7), while Ring and Anning (2004) stress children's use of drawing to 're-present action, emotion, ideas or experience and tell complex stories'. The use of drawing in art therapy is based 'on the accepted belief that drawings represent the inner psychological realities and the subjective experiences of the person who creates the images' (Malchiodi, 1998:5).

Accordingly, the research methodology explored within this book sought to use visual arts workshops as a way of engaging with the experiences of young children. My thinking has also been influenced by the ideas of Eileen Adams, a key figure of the 'Campaign for Drawing', which originated in the UK in 1999 with the objective of demonstrating why drawing should be more highly valued in education and everyday life. Writing about the potential of drawing when working with young people, Adams notes how it

> can be used as a tool of enquiry, comprehension and communication. It enables young people to order and understand their experiences, to shape ideas and to communicate their thinking and feeling to others. (2002:222)

One of the challenges for teachers, artists and other cultural workers is to find ways of actively engaging children with the arts in a manner that does not educationalise perceptions of the art form but instead allows children to engage more deeply on critical and creative levels. Structured investigation through drawing is one possible approach. This chapter briefly discusses the

Figure 9.1: Lost in drawing. A research workshop in progress.
Photograph by Brian Hartley.

possible ways of using drawing in relation to a theatre experience before providing examples of the ways in which it enhances the experience through memory, observation, interpretation and invention.

But I can't draw!

Many adults are actively scared of drawing or of being asked to draw. Many adults would instinctively assert that they 'can't draw'. However, it is important to remember that the role of drawing in this context is not about skill or accuracy, although it is certainly about trying and doing your best. Instead it is primarily about expression and exploring the different expressive qualities of drawing and the different insights that can be discovered through drawing something rather than talking about it.

Unlike adults, most children will happily draw and will relish opportunities for free drawing if they have generous and rich materials. Some children might struggle because they have been told by an adult that they can't draw. The complaint that 'I can't draw' is heard mostly from adults but is unfortunately echoed by some children, particularly from about the age of nine, when children began to judge their own drawings according to rigid criteria of representational realism. Disappointed with their products and abilities, and sometimes, alas, accepting the unkind judgements of others that they cannot draw, children of this age may abandon drawing altogether (Malchiodi, 1998:91-96). A gap develops between what Matthews calls 'competence and performance' (1999:94) as a child's drawing abilities inevitably fail to match up to their desired or imagined representation: they cannot realise their mental picture as well as they would like. For younger children this is seldom a problem but for older children it can be crippling.

The gap between competence and performance can cause children to adopt particular drawing strategies and choices. They might change their drawings and their own articulations and understandings of them as they produce them. For example, in one workshop some of the children were struggling to draw a picture of the goose: one girl who was disappointed with her drawing decided it was a duck instead; a boy transformed his misshaped goose into a toy plane ('Yeah because I was going to draw the bird but then it went wrong so it's going to be a toy plane'). In response to a different production, one boy discovered as he reached the end of a drawing that he did not have room for the hundreds of dogs demanded by the story, but only for one. The explanation he invented was that one dog could run faster than the rest, so the others were left behind and therefore out of the picture.

So the responses to the gap between competence and performance in drawing can be discouraging for children or alternatively it can be seen as playful and liberating. In every case it is vital that children know we are not interested in the relative accuracy of their drawings, but in their creative and expressive content. And the best way to do this is for adults to model our own good or not so good drawing abilities.

It is useful to begin a drawing workshop with tasks that cause the participants to forget about their artistic abilities or lack of them and simply start making marks on paper, such as drawing a continuous line without taking the pen off the paper, drawing with the wrong hand or with the eyes closed. Such externally imposed limitations provide a focus for the exercise that is separate from the quality and content of the drawing. Or the task might be to draw holding a long bamboo cane to which is taped a pen, pencil or paint brush. The resultant pictures are less inhibited by a desire to 'get it right' so are more expressive and communicative.

Drawing as knowledge

Once children have drawn a picture of the performance they have watched, what next? Getting children to draw, as most teachers or parents generally do, is just the first stage. The pictures are then briefly admired, displayed on the wall or perhaps posted to the theatre company. But these pictures can be used as the basis for exploratory conversation or reflection. Engaging the children in conversation about the drawings allows the processes, thinking and knowledge behind the pictures to emerge (see the questioning technique discussed in Chapter Four).

The insights that can emerge in the drawing process warrant further consideration. As it is often the teacher, parent or art worker's role to facilitate and ease out these insights, it is useful to have an idea of what to look for in the drawings and what tacit knowledge might lie within the images.

Through a series of booklets published by Power Drawing, Adams has articulated how drawings are used, not least by children, as a means of ordering, exploration and experimentation (Adams and Baynes, 2003). Adams indicates the rich potential of examining children's knowledge and experience through drawings. I have drawn on her work in developing the following analysis of the ways in which drawing can be a form of looking, a way of learning and of interpreting the experience of a theatre performance. I have structured this in four parts: memory, observation, interpretation and invention (see also table 9.1).

Memory

- Drawing helps us make sense of an experience.

- A drawing is a trace of an experience, through which we can re-work and understand our memory more fully.

- Drawing assists the ordering of sensations, feelings, ideas and thoughts.

Observation

- Drawing helps us look more closely and think about what we have seen.

- Through drawing we can investigate and learn about the qualities of what we have seen – whether that is shape, structure, pattern, texture, the play of light or the position of an object in space.

Interpretation

- In revealing to us what we have seen, drawing can help us go beyond the naming of parts to arrive at the underlying qualities of a scene or the essence of a character.

- Drawing helps us reflect upon and interpret experience and perhaps achieve new insights.

Invention

- Drawing develops ideas, from embryonic stage to form.

- Sometimes an idea emerges from the drawn marks.

- Sometimes invention is the result of happy accident, an unintentional mark or spill.

- Through drawing we can add and change, create new relationships and scenarios.

Table 9.1: Drawing as a form of knowledge
(Based upon Adams and Baynes, 2003)

Memory

Adams suggests that drawing helps us make sense of an experience, allowing us to order sensations, feelings, ideas and thoughts. More practically, but as importantly, drawing is an activity that takes time, providing space for reflection and recollection:

Researcher: So are you thinking about what you want to draw?

Eilidh: Ahemm.

Researcher: Well, what do you remember?

Eilidh: I remember lots of things, but I just don't know what to draw.

Researcher: What did you like about the show?

Eilidh: Emmm.

Interjection by another pupil: Eilidh's really embarrassed sometimes.

Researcher: I'm sorry, would it help, do you want to just start drawing and I'll go away then, yes? OK.

A drawing has to be started somewhere, and this is not always easy to decide. However, as the extract above suggests, it is a decision that has a different and more private dynamic than that demanded by an immediate, verbal response. And once that initial decision on where to start and what to draw has been made, then the picture evolves and changes as it is produced: Eilidh did not talk much, but she did produce an elaborate, reflective and detailed drawing that said much about the complex and subtle ways in which she remembered the experience. A particular advantage of drawing over other creative task-based activities such as video making or drama is that it is immediate. This makes it especially suitable when working with children.

What children might be thinking when they begin a drawing, and the processes of memory and reflection that continue in the time it takes them to complete their work, may be reflected in their final pictures but is unavailable to explicit knowledge. It becomes most apparent when children draw and talk at the same time, as in this exchange about the puppeteer in *Psst!*:

Max: And I saw the man with the wig on his head.

Researcher: The man with the wig on his head? I don't remember a man with a wig on his head, do you want to tell me more?

Max: No wig on his head, I know that guy. I can draw him. No he's a big guy, he needs the puppets...

Researcher: And what did you think it was on his head?

Max: A brick.

Researcher: A brick on his head...?

Max: One, two, three, four, five...I'm just counting my hands. No he's not a puppet.

Researcher: He's not a puppet...

Max: He makes the puppet move. I know that guy.

Max provides a commentary on his drawing as he draws, and the experience and knowledge of that experience is brought back to his mind by the act of drawing.

The act of drawing encourages children to recall ever greater detail about what they saw and requires the children to test their abilities of recall. This is particularly the case with a production that deliberately uses the careful accumulation of small details and props to construct meaning or communicate something about character or place. Many of the children taking part in my research delighted in this, filling their pictures with observational detail. One child, for example, remarked when asked if he had finished a picture of Martha's house, 'I think I'm going to do a wee bit more detail for the rubbish and sea'. Interestingly, it had not been this detail that the children had first articulated as memorable about the performance, but it was clearly remembered and replicated in their drawings.

The process of drawing the performance, therefore, both extends and changes the nature of children's engagement with the performance they saw. In the first instance, this is through factual memory and memory of details – a kind of naming of parts – and this initial comprehension of what was seen is vital. Importantly in drawing, and creative representation more generally, this initial process of uncovering memory also encourages other and different kinds of knowing.

Observation

Uncovering what was seen through drawing involves utilising observation. However, drawing also requires that we look or reflect more closely and think about what we have seen. Eileen Adams suggests that through drawing we can investigate and learn about the qualities of what we have seen – whether that is shape, structure, pattern, texture or purpose – in a way that becomes a form of thinking.

This observation is manifested in the ways in which children's drawings require them to represent the things seen in the performance. We can see an exploration of colour and to some extent shape in a drawing by Evan (figure 9.2) which includes a depiction of the large structure that featured on one side of the stage during the performance of *Psst!* This was a slightly ambiguous object, all white and covered in a lacy fabric that reflected the light in different ways. At first it looked as if it was part of one of the puppeteer's costume, although she was in fact standing inside the structure. Later it was used as a table. Several of the children picked up on the ornate frills and layered effect and called it a 'cake thing'.

What is significant is that Evan did not know exactly what this object was. He did not have a name by which to label and identify it and tell him how to draw it via a representational schema. So when he is asked about his drawing, he answers ambiguously and focuses on colour:

> **Researcher**: What's this big shape, Evan?
>
> **Evan**: It was that white bit, it was that white bit where the lady was at. I was going put white over it.

And while he draws the object Evan continues to think about colour and the challenge of how to depict the different shades of white he saw on the white paper he is using – 'I think I could use a different colour of white than that, like a different kind of shade of white'. In seeking to do this, Evan is prompted by a workshop facilitator to consider using bits of paper of different shades of white. Left alone, he spends several minutes cutting out this paper and sticking it down in the layered and subtle manner of his drawing. This not only represents the different shades of white that he saw, but also the textured character of the fabric.

Although responding to the workshop facilitator, who was able to direct him in terms of materials, it was Evan himself who made the observation of the object's primary characteristic: whiteness. It was Evan who set himself the challenge, the need to represent different shades of white, and who produced the representation. And it was Evan who found this subtle and complex manner of representation suitable for his experience. The interaction between seeing and the representation of that seeing is complex. But the process of producing this representation, with a guiding hand, certainly helped Evan to see and understand more about what he had seen. The process provides an interesting model for extending and deepening children's engagement with performances through art practice.

The example Evan provides is particularly striking but other instances presented similar explorations of colour, such as Ruaridh's painting of a palm tree surrounded by a dense, glowing yellow:

Figure 9.2: The cake thing by Evan

Researcher: Hello Ruaridh, that's a very yellow drawing.

Ruaridh: Umm, it's the sunlight spreading.

Researcher: Ah, why is there so much sunlight?

Ruaridh: Because it's really really hot, because I was imagining it was in the summer in Africa.

Elsewhere in his conversation Ruaridh refers to this sunlight several times, at another point saying 'Yeah I'm going to be doing the sunlight and the sky. Sunlight here as well.' It is clearly a central factor of his drawing, as important to him as the other, more narrative content. What he has found is a representational device that allows him to extend the evocative moment of the story, which featured references to a desert and the hot sun. The bright, atmospheric and entirely appropriate yellowness, however, never appeared on stage. It is all Ruaridh's. It is the product of his imaginative engagement with the question of how to complete the moment begun in the performance.

Other examples include children who used drawing as an observational practice through which to engage with more technical aspects of the production. In response to *Psst!*, for example, Robert responded by drawing it as seen from above, producing a stage plan and a number of cut-out figures which could be moved around to perform the action. Kristofer produced an overhead view of the stage and auditorium; Fraser drew a representation of how one puppet was operated, including a cut-away to what might be happening underneath the stage; while several of the children cut their figures out, as if producing little puppets of their own. It is speculative but reasonable to suggest that with *Psst!* the recurring interest in cutting out was motivated partly by the desire to mimic the 3D form of the puppets. Visual art offered a particular opportunity to do this, enabling the children to test their observations as they explored the form of the puppets and how things worked and fitted together.

Different productions require different kinds of knowing and invite different responses; the flexibility of visual art allows a range of representational engagement that enhance different kinds of observation. Aspects of this have to do with the visual skills children bring to their engagement with the performances. It was noticeable that children with strong artistic skills seemed to remember more and see more. The relationships between visual knowing and drawing are, as Adams asserts, strong and are part of a broad visual literacy that is largely neglected within schools.

Interpretation

With theatre, not all the information or representation appears on the stage; much is left to the audience's imagination. For the production to make sense, the audience may be required to lend their imagination. This can be considered to be a process of interpretation, where the audience gathers together the clues provided and establishes some kind of conclusion about the nature of the experience, the essence of a character, the qualities of a scene. The process of visual representation allows this to occur, providing opportunities to reflect upon and interpret the experience and achieve new insights.

This was particularly the case with *Them With Tails*, where much of the performance had no material structure or form and the drawings were therefore about the interpretation and fleshing out of stage information. As already discussed, the large majority of the children's drawings of this production depicted not what they had seen but what they had imagined – or more accurately, what they imagined when they were engaged in the process of making the drawing. Importantly, it is only when called upon to make a drawing that the children had to think about *exactly* how the things described to them might have looked.

Some of the children resolved this challenge by adopting what can be described as 'representational schema' or production of conventionalised drawings. Reflection on the use of drawing and painting in art therapy explores how a child's developmental stage in drawing produces various kinds of recurring motifs, conventionalisations and standardisations in representation. A child's expectations of form (what a drawing is, conventionally), of materials (such as what it means to use paint) and of subject (such as what a particular thing is) can lead them to produce certain kinds of representations. One fairly straightforward example of the use of representational schema is how children conventionally include a round yellow circle and blue sky in their drawings to represent a sunny day. An exchange with a child about her drawing ran along the following lines:

> **Researcher**: And lovely blue sky at the top of yours.
>
> **Maneeba**: The sun next to it too.
>
> **Researcher**: Was it a sunny day in the story?
>
> **Maneeba**: I just drew it.

Children often started by drawing the sun in a top corner of the paper before even deciding what the rest of the picture would consist of. And in some depictions of a scene that took place indoors, a sunny day representation is still included. However, while Maneeba unreflectively drew a sunny day as part of an automatic representational schema, other children were also able to talk about and rationalise *why* they had included the sun and *how* they had gathered this information. While the visual depiction remained conventionalised, they could articulate why they had drawn the sunny day representation (see Chapter Six).

In children's drawings and those of many adults, we can see a range of ways in which schema are utilised to depict things that are known and understood through conventionalised representations. For example, in one of the productions there was a verbal description of bubbles made by a crocodile hiding underwater. Several children, working separately or in groups, produced fairly similar depictions of the bubbles as small o's. This is easily identifiable as our representational schema for bubbles, recognisable from all sorts of depictions, including cartoons, illustrated stories, advertisements and more besides. The children's drawings of bubbles, constructed within a representational schema, were entirely appropriate, and demonstrated their ability to call upon known signifiers to flesh out the world imaginatively evoked for them. One interesting question is whether it was these drawn, schematic bubbles that the children imagined during the performance, or if they only materialised when they were called upon to produce a pictorial image.

So it is interesting to identify the kinds of interpretations at play in children's drawings. The difference between the use of representational schema of sunny-day-ness, and deliberate and conscious choice in representation, is subtle but very telling. It can only be fully understood through matching the children's drawings with their talk about the drawings. It is possible to identify the children's active engagement with known representational marks, as in the instance of bubbles, as a method of interpreting their experience. Particularly noticeable are those moments when the children actively break away from known representational schema and start to make conscious and distinctive choices of their own.

This is most strikingly apparent in the instances where the children were faced with the task of drawing something they did not fully understand. For example, one of the stories in *Them With Tails* was about a basilisk. None of the children knew what a basilisk looked like and, in a production without full costumes, they had to rely on a stage presentation that merely incorporated a couple of feathers and a red coxcomb-like headdress. In their drawings of this creature, most of the children responded by latching onto its bird-like qualities and drawing an assortment of monstrous chickens.

Figure 9.3: Something evil in this drawing by Ben

The intriguing, if largely unanswerable, question is whether during the performance the children completed the evoked experience in their own imagination *as they watched*. While we can be fairly certain that they were thinking of the basilisk while watching the performance, it was probably in a nebulous and fluctuating form. What is almost certain is that during the performance they did not see something as evolved, detailed and complete as that which they produced in their drawings. When watching the performance, Caley surely did not imagine the striking and colourful bird-creature she drew, or Megan her giant singing chicken. Rather, this imagination of the basilisk was produced through the process of drawing.

Ben (figure 9.3) accurately remembered the basilisk's ability to turn people into stone and had an understanding of this in terms of the creature's symbolic meaning within the play. But he adds details of his own to this, appropriately and playfully, saying: 'I'm doing something evil in this drawing' and described his creature's giant ears, cheeks which can fire lasers and 'hands which can make the sky half darkness, half lightness'. Ben's memorial engagement with the production took place within the realms of language and drawing, and of factual recall, reflection and imaginative re-construction. Clearly though, because of this process, the experience started to resonate in his memory beyond the duration of the production.

Within the flow of watching a performance the imagination does not have to be fixed and concrete. It can be fluid and variable, changing from one instance to the next. This is particularly so with described detail, which the audience only needs to realise imaginatively in a sketchy fashion when it is evoked. The audience can simply add detail to their mental picture as they learn it, over-writing any previous imaginative image. During the actual performance, the children were required to know only two things about the basilisk: firstly, that semiotically it was represented by feathers, a red headdress and a funny walk; and secondly, in terms of plot, that it was an evil monster that turned people into stone. Nothing else mattered.

In contrast, drawing requires us to come up with a particular, concrete visualisation that is all there and fully realised. This applied to everything in the performance, with drawing a process of thinking and reflecting which required the children to consider exactly what it was they had seen or imagined. While the children knew what, for example, a princess was, exactly what this *particular* princess looked like was something they only had to decide when putting pen or pencil to paper.

This might suggest that asking the children to produce a drawing of the perfor-mance bore little relation to their theatre experience – they did not literally see the performance in the same way they drew it. Yet it is clear from the children's willingness to participate in the endeavour that these completed visual images, while not constructed during the actual performance, are central to the children's conscious and reflective encountering of it. This points to an unconscious, assumed or unnoticed ability to attend to the performance on various levels as required – to read the surface layer of signs in order to follow the performance, and to dig down into the denotative and connotative mean-ings of these signs as required. It also points to the value and importance of providing children with a structure through which they can work through their memories and perceptions after the event.

Invention

I have discussed the representation and imagination of things not literally there on the stage but determinately there in the world of the theatrical experience. However, once a production begins to utilise children's imagination in order to complete the performance and make it meaningful, it is difficult to put a stop on that imagination and the playful impulses it produces. And as long as the responses are working within the parameters set up by the performance, it is difficult to label any imaginative response as right or wrong, even if it begins to produce things not included within the referential world presented by the performance itself.

So, for example, Lorraine produced a drawing of a mermaid, a character that did occur in one story told in *Them With Tails*, but it is joined in her picture by seaweed, a fish and an octopus. I remember talking to her about this drawing and being perplexed by the presence of the octopus: there was not one in the play; what was it doing there, I asked? The answer I received was so obvious that only a dumb adult could not have got it: mermaids live underwater, octopuses live underwater therefore...

While neither there on stage nor directly referenced by the production, these details were entirely appropriate within the connotative world of the performance. Their invention is within the frame of the performance; they are supportive to the key referent of the mermaid and her underwater palace, and also to the anarchic style of the production. Yet although appropriate, they are not directly referentially there, so require a willingness to stretch the boundaries of the production and the truth of what happened. Lorraine is not limiting herself to the confines of her literal memory; our own understanding of this needs to be more subtle than only the accuracy of recall.

Drawing encourages play of this kind. Asking the children to produce a drawing required them to add to what was given to them by the production. And, in doing more, they came to realise that they had a kind of playful power over the production. As they made their choices in representation, they came to control what they had seen. Moreover, while we cannot be certain what the children saw in their mind's eye as they watched the performance, we can be fairly certain that it is these drawings that determined what will be remembered from this point onwards.

The act of reflection and representation thus begins to instil a kind of ownership of the experience: as we draw, we have actively to contribute to that experience. This is what we have to do while watching – for the performance is not complete, but borrows on the imagination of its audience – but the representational process makes this movement explicit, concrete and fully realised.

One final example of this is the series of drawings produced by two boys working side by side. In these pictures, Ajay and Alasdair have imagined Bob the Sumo wrestler, a character in one of the stories told in *Them With Tails* (figure 9.4). The boys began their representation where one might expect, depicting the huge size that forms our known representational schema of sumo wrestlers:

Researcher: Who's this guy you've drawn?

Ajay: Em, Bob.

Researcher: This is Ajay's drawing of Bob.

Ajay: He's a sumo, he's a sumo.

Researcher: Sumo! And you know what a sumo wrestler looks like obviously?

Ajay: Yeah he has, he has.

Researcher: 'Cause you've drawn one.

Ajay: He's got a big tummy and they, they do this [gestures, stamps foot on the floor].

Figure 9.4: Muscles on muscles by Alasdair. The figures along the bottom are Bob's army of flying pigs.

This is what they drew first. As they continued to spend time and creative energy on their drawing, they added less expected elements, such as the way they drew the muscles:

Researcher: What are all these?

Alasdair: Five storey muscles.

Ajay: He's got bigger ones.

Researcher: Oh, huge muscles!

Ajay: What is that?

Alasdair: Muscles.

Researcher: Muscles on muscles.

And even muscles in surprising places:

Researcher: He is so muscley! You've both got muscles.

Alasdair: And he's got muscles on his eyes.

Researcher: Muscles on his eyes [laughs].

Ajay: There!

Alasdair: That's why they're green.

Here the two boys have started from the point provided for them in the performance, but with the crucial impetus that this was not completed in itself. The performance did not provide a fully realised representation of a sumo wrestler – the boys have taken flight with the ideas and made them their own. Part of the stimulation came from working in partnership, but the act of drawing and the period of time taken by the drawing was just as important. The first impulse was the position provided for them, the last was their own. And although it was their own, it was entirely appropriate in terms of both the narrative and style of the production itself.

This instance is amongst the most visually developed examples of the way in which imaginative play with the ideas of the production can both extend engagement and establish a clear sense of ownership of the experiences. But it was apparent in many of the children's drawings. The children's relationship with the performance often evolved through the process of drawing: through the time, reflection, craft and creativity that drawing requires; and through engagement with memory, observation, interpretation and invention. This does not mean that the nature of engagement can be planned or structured, on the part of either the children or the workshop leaders. But it is this kind of playful reflection that drawing encourages.

10

Talking about Theatre

Talking about a performance after the event can be as significant to the experience of theatre as the production itself. We have the urge to talk about the performance, to share memories, interpretations and experiences. It is almost an itch that must be scratched, a need that must be fulfilled. This is true not only of theatre; we often feel the need to talk about the experience of any artistic event. We have the sense that art needs to be interpreted, discussed and re-communicated after we experience it in order to complete that experience. With theatre the need to talk about the experience is heightened by the time-based and ephemeral nature of the performance and by the social nature of the event.

Yet talking about a performance after the event is often frustrating. The post-performance conversation usually begins with the familiar, stilted and almost archetypal opening questions – 'what did you think?' or 'did you enjoy it?' – that almost inevitably means we are not given the chance to explore the subtlety and complexity of the performance just experienced.

Language itself can be frustrating. Although it is powerful and flexible, there are certain things that we feel are ineffable: things we feel we know, experience, remember but just cannot put into words. This is perhaps particularly true for young children, whose vocabulary and speech may fail to keep up with the speed of their thought processes and desire to communicate.

So although it may be natural and instinctive, the successful consummation of the post-show conversation cannot be taken for granted. This chapter explores talking about theatre, and then examines possible models that provide a structure or critical methodology for talking about art. How can young children's critical engagement with theatre be encouraged in a way that enhances, deepens and broadens the pleasures of their experience?

The need to talk about art

The idea that we have an ingrained need to talk about our art experiences is recognised within many art forms. Literary critic Norman Holland, for example, notes the need for communication about literature, suggesting that we want more than the personal experience, we also want peers (1981:242); which perhaps explains some of the popularity of book groups. Similarly, art critic Edmund Burke Feldman describes the 'desire to share what we have found. It is very difficult to know or enjoy something without thinking about the reactions of someone else' (1992:469).

While this urge to talk about the experience can exist with essentially private forms such as the novel, with arts which are experienced in a social setting – such as theatre or dance – the desire to externalise the experience is intensified. The social nature of theatre can be thought of as intersubjective: it is a space where proximity, shared focus and the very architecture of the building means that we become acutely aware of the existence of others. Intersubjectivity equates to the 'thereness-for-me' of others, a phenomenological concept expressed in Jean-Paul Sartre's observation that during a performance 'each member of an audience asks himself what he thinks of a play and at the same time what his neighbour is thinking' (1976: 67).

Two points are worth underlining in this consideration of theatre audiences. First, audience members ask themselves what they are thinking: the performance is there to be experienced, to be responded to, and to be thought about. Like all art, it is an event that focuses attention, which underlines its own significances. One does not normally ask oneself what one thinks about the experience of, for instance, walking down the street – which is not typically presented or perceived as an experience of significance – but the question is instinctive in relation to art because its presentational aspect is always conspicuous. Secondly, audience members ask what their neighbours are thinking. Live performance is a social event: prompting not just the individual's awareness of others but also an awareness of the personal responses of others. The strong community aspect of live performance creates a desire to share responses and externalise the experience. As Ubersfeld writes, theatre is rarely a solitary pleasure, but rather is 'reflected on and reverberates through others' (1982:128). One teenage theatre-goer speaks for the kind of motives and impulses that are going on:

> **Natalie**: I'd just feel silly if I went to the theatre alone, altho' many do, and there shouldn't be a stigma attached to it – doing most things alone basically make it look like you've got no friends – when that's a rather juvenile way of looking

at it. But, also, it's great to have someone to discuss things with, and ask questions, and express to how much you loved or hated something.

Clearly, there is a social aspect to going to and talking about live performance with friends. But the role of the post-show conversation is more than just social, as Natalie implies. It provides an opportunity to 'ask questions' about the performance just seen. Post-performance conversation affords the opportunity to check and compare what it was we just saw. Once one leaves the theatre performance, such conversations represent the only method of affirming our memory of the event. Dance critic Deborah Jowitt links this to the transience of live performance, writing that 'people like to talk about dances afterwards in order to prolong their [the dances'] ephemeral existence' (1977: 101). The same applies to theatre. There is, then, an urgency to talk about live performance that is grounded in the need to affirm one's memory of the event; the post-show conversation is a way of exploring one overarching concern, namely 'what was it we just saw?'

The value of critical engagement

Some might argue that even such informal and instinctive conversations, let alone critical study or discussion, can deaden the experience of theatre. Similarly, some claim that too much knowledge about theatre dampens or distances the power of the thing itself. What does it matter if we cannot say more? That we cannot find the words? That our responses are limited to articulations of simple pleasures and likes or dislikes? Perhaps part of the thrill of the aesthetic experience is that it is beyond words.

On the contrary, I maintain that increased knowledge increases engagement and intensifies the pleasures and satisfactions associated with engagement with the arts. We saw in Chapter Six how children demonstrated pleasure in their ability to read and analyse the workings of a performance. This pleasure of understanding – which is also a pleasure of knowledge – enhances children's ability and willingness to engage with the theatrical experience. It enables them to see and remember more; it makes the experience mean more to them.

Pleasure in understanding is only one of the many ways in which audiences gain pleasure from a performance but it is a very important one. Crucially, it is also an empowering pleasure, at it places the audience in an active, commanding and interpreting position. This is in contrast to emotional or empathetic pleasures, where the audience are in many ways at the mercy and manipulation of the performance. The ability of knowledge and criticality to give us authority over our own experiences is vital, especially for young audiences.

Critical discussion about the theatrical experience, therefore, should be both empowering and pleasurable. Feldman usefully brings these two qualities together when he describes the pleasure of understanding as one of the functions of art criticism:

> We get pleasure from understanding, from knowing what it is in art that causes our gratification. The trained viewer should also be able to experience more of the satisfactions a work is capable of yielding; criticism enables us to carry on the search systematically. The satisfactions we get from art depend on two things: the quality of the object itself, and our capacity to use our own experience in seeing it. So art criticism increases pleasure while teaching us to focus our knowledge and experience in an aesthetic situation. (1992:469)

For Feldman, art criticism is talk about art that has a degree of informed structure and should form a legitimate and valuable part of young children's art education. Yet this does not exist within schools, nor is it necessarily easy to foster. As Martha Taunton writes:

> Teaching art through provocative dialogue is particularly difficult for those who teach preschool and early elementary age children. In part, this difficulty simply stems from a lack of realisation and faith that young children can and should discuss art in a meaningful way, but, in part, it often results from uncertainty about how to conduct discussions about art with children who are so young. (1983:40)

A range of models exists that might be applied to enabling young children to gain increased artistic pleasure through art criticism.

Philosophy for Children

A conceptually and practically developed approach to engaging young children in thinking about the world through dialogue is Philosophy for Children (P4C). The discussion that follows was developed through research funded by Imaginate into the possible use of P4C to facilitate and enhance post-theatre discussion in schools (for a fuller discussion see Reason, 2008).

Matthew Lipman first developed philosophy for children in the United States in the 1970s and it has been significantly adapted in the UK, particularly since the 1990s. Its methodology and ethos seek to encourage and enable children's critical and independent thinking. It is about enhancing thinking skills, including the ability to think for oneself, weigh up evidence and challenge received opinions through scrutiny and reasoning. Importantly, however, it is seen as not just a part of teaching but as a revolutionary act in the context of schools where pupils are not equal with teachers and compulsory education provides a real obstacle to freedom of thought and of the individual (Haynes, 2002:2).

P4C sessions consist of child-led explorations and enquiries. According to Joanna Haynes, the teacher, if genuinely committed to the enquiry and able to resist the natural urge to lead the discussion, does not know the content of the enquiry in advance, as it is determined by the children. This is a challenge in an education system where the emphasis is on obtaining precise objectives and outcomes (Haynes, 2002:28). But the P4C session is not a free-for-all. It takes the form of a structured enquiry focused around a particular stimulus material. Within this structure there are five key stages to a P4C session: 1) sharing the stimulus material; 2) thinking time; 3) development of questions; 4) selection of question; 5) dialogue.

Thus P4C sessions begin with the introduction of the stimulus material, such as a story that is read out aloud in the class. The selection of the stimulus is vital to the success of the subsequent discussion. Haynes points out that teachers need to 'select materials carefully on the basis of their power to express ambiguity, to produce puzzlement or to evoke a deep response' (2002: 22). Originally, P4C session in America were based on materials that were written specifically for the purpose: stories highlighting philosophical questions for the children to explore. The British application has tended not to use such material and instead employs found stimuli, particularly picture books but also poems, music, photographs, art objects (Liptai, 2005:1-2) or – as in my own research – theatre.

P4C positively values the inquisitiveness and creativity children bring to thinking, and seeks to encourage this and the process of enquiry over the valuation of facts and answers. Gareth Matthews suggests that in areas such as 'conceptual play', wonderment and fancy (playing 'what if') young children can take great delight in the kind of questioning that is central to philosophy. He fears, however, that 'adults discourage children from asking philosophical questions, first by being patronising to them and then by directing their minds to more 'useful' investigations' (Matthews, 1980:73).

A key element of P4C is that the children themselves formulate and select the question that will form the basis of the enquiry. This stage often takes up a substantial part of each session in the case of found rather than purpose-made stimuli, where it is not so much a matter of formulating questions as finding them. P4C views the development of questions as not just a necessary stage in the pursuit of answers but as a fundamental part of the process of thinking. The objective is for the children to develop their own questions, but these must be philosophical rather than factual or memory based. The children develop a sense of what kind of questions are needed. Children in one P4C session I observed provided the following list of criteria to define what a philosophical question might be:

'There isn't a right or wrong answer.'
'It is a question that there is no answer to.'
'Sometimes you need to use your imagination.'
'You have to do your opinion, not somebody else's.'
'Try not to ask questions that you can answer.'

Philip Cam offers this diagram of different kinds of questions:

Look and see	Questions for thinking
Ask an expert	Use your imagination

'Look and see' questions are those where you can find the answer by examining the original source. 'Ask an expert' questions are those which have a clear answer you could obtain by asking the appropriate person. In contrast, the categories on the right of the chart are areas where there are no clear right or wrong answers and where debate might be genuinely philosophical. There is clearly tension within P4C between wanting to allow the questions to emerge from the children themselves, according to their own interests and engagements, and wanting to direct them towards questions that are indeed philosophical. The teacher's position is immensely tricky: it is located between being a facilitator and a leader; between keeping certain objectives in mind, while also striving to ensure the empowerment of the children.

Once the question is selected, the final stage of a P4C enquiry is the dialogue, the discussion intended to address the question. This is led and to a large extent chaired by the children themselves. Although often very divergent and free flowing, what stops these sessions from descending into chaos are the various structures and devices that the P4C facilitator can use and pass on to the children. As Haynes puts it, 'the teacher models the language of philosophical discourse and introduces conceptual tools to extend or to record the development of ideas' (2002:12). The most basic of these understandings modelled by the teacher is the nature of a debate: it is not acceptable simply to state one's opinion or to dismiss somebody else's; evidence and argument have to be presented to support what is said.

Another device used to structure debate is that pupils record their agreement or disagreement with each other's statements. Sometimes this is done through a vote by the whole group: thumbs up, thumbs down, or sideways for uncertainty; sometimes through counter statements. So a pupil might say 'I disagree with X' and then be required to say how and why, providing evidence for their statements. In my experience, there are times when the children's decisions on whether to agree or disagree appear to be motivated by friendship or other factors; sometimes the responses are jokingly personal – in one session a girl responded to a disagreement with 'are you fighting with me?'; on another occasion a girl said to a friend 'that's twice you've disagreed with me, it's outrageous'. But on the whole this structure allows discussion to be intellectual rather than personal. One significant marker of this for me is when children change their mind as a result of what others have said, publicly noting that they *had* changed their minds and why. This altering of opinion during the course of a discussion, and being consciously aware of how and why, is clear evidence of engagement on a critical level.

What is striking from observing P4C sessions in action is that the children have internalised the codes and structures of the discussion, such as the idea of what a philosophical question is, or the notion of evidence or of structured discussion. This comes about through experience of the process of P4C, through building up a community of enquiry and through the examples of good practice modelled by the teacher. In this sense, then, each philosophical enquiry does not begin with the sharing of the stimulus but is part of an ongoing process within a community. This concept of a community of enquiry is central to P4C, with ideas and values introduced explicitly at the outset but then adopted implicitly and consistently by the participants themselves.

I have observed that these kinds of values – listening carefully, not interrupting, respecting each other – are implicit in the sessions, with the children only occasionally having to be reminded of them. At times the children would even correct each other if somebody strayed from the codes of behaviour. For example, it was expected that the children address their arguments to each other and not the teacher; one girl corrected another who was talking to the facilitator by saying 'you're supposed to be saying stuff to us'. Not that the sessions were always calm, with no interruptions and everyone listening carefully – but these values were at least understood. P4C is a process of working with children that takes place over a long period of regular meetings, so allowing the pupils to internalise the process. It cannot simply be started and stopped.

From philosophy enquiry to aesthetic enquiry

Although it has many impressive qualities, there are elements of P4C that do not match those required for an aesthetic enquiry that might follow a theatre performance. P4C imposes restrictions, which is rather ironic for an approach that celebrates its revolutionary ambition of empowering children through philosophy.

In demanding that questions be 'philosophical', P4C disallows many of the questions that naturally follow a theatre performance: about what was seen; checking details; sharing memories. It is with such questions that children generally want to begin, asking seemingly banal questions about frustratingly insignificant details. I think such questions are required, since children are concerned first with understanding the experience, and need to do so before they move on to more abstract philosophical or aesthetic questioning. I thank Sara Liptai, a P4C practitioner who has conducted enquiries into music, for helping me reach this formulation. One example she provided was how, after she read children the New Testament parable of *The Workers in the Vineyard*, they wanted to dwell at length on the type of coinage ('talents') used to reward the workers and how unfair it was that all workers received the same payment irrespective of the length of their working day. Liptai explains that 'when [children] ask us for such details they want to understand the context and the rules of the genre' (personal communication). In this specific context, the ephemeral nature of theatre possibly adds to this element, with the children first having to understand what had happened.

In P4C the stimulus material is used as the starting point that is subsequently discarded in the pursuit of abstract discussions and ideas. As Liptai writes:

> In conventional enquiry the (purpose-written philosophical) text is the springboard for enquiry: a vehicle, and no more than that, to convey the participants to the realm of PI [Philosophical Inquiry]. The text is not, or is not meant to have, intrinsic aesthetic qualities. (2005:3)

Liptai suggests in a footnote that for the pioneer of P4C, Matthew Lipman, such aesthetic qualities would have been a distraction from the business of philosophy. However, a picture, a piece of music or a theatre production have in contrast, clear aesthetic qualities. They have a coherence or sustained existence and meaning outside the classroom in a way that is not the case with purpose written philosophical source texts. For Liptai, the significance of this aesthetic quality for P4C is that 'a work of art refuses to be used as just a springboard for the emerging philosophical ideas and then to be abandoned' (2005:5). Thus a shift is needed from a philosophical enquiry that leaves the stimulus material behind to an aesthetic enquiry that begins by digging deeper into the stimulus itself.

In developing the concept of aesthetic enquiry with children, Liptai raises some tensions with key elements of P4C practice. For example, she suggests that in aesthetic enquiry 'it is necessary to understand the prevailing cultural conventions, ie the rules of the genre' and also the work's cultural and historical environment (2005:4). Yet it is unclear where this knowledge comes from if the teacher continues to play the role of facilitator rather than expert, or has to play simultaneous roles, at once instructor and facilitator. We see this tension in another paper on non-text-based aesthetic enquiry, where Liptai observes that

> Some children use musical vocabulary (eg soft, getting louder) but most children construct their own way of expressing musical (and pictorial) meaning, unhindered by the absence of such vocabulary. However, the next stage in their development could well be moving towards a more specific and professional vocabulary by investigating the components of the musical meanings they have identified. (2004:5)

Aside from the role of the teacher in such an enquiry, this discussion raises the question of whether specialist knowledge and vocabulary is required in responses to art or whether uninformed responses are equally valid. From my own work with young theatre audiences, I would add that the ability to utilise specialist knowledge gives children, and indeed adults, a particular kind of pleasure and therefore enhances both their investment in the experience and the experience itself.

What children require following a theatrical experience, therefore, is a particular kind of aesthetic rather than philosophical enquiry that directs, focuses and deepens their own responses and experiences. In order to do this, children need to be provided with the language and structure of theatrical enquiry designed to sharpen and develop insights into the stimulus itself. It is precisely the 'look and see' questions, which come on the left-hand side of Philip Cam's diagram and which are discarded as non-philosophical, with which I would suggest any engagement with art should begin.

Models from the visual arts

The area which has seen the greatest activity in the development of models of aesthetic enquiry, particularly those designed for children, is that of the visual arts. There are a number of reasons why activity is more strongly advanced in this area than in theatre or other performing arts, namely the accessibility and reproducibility of the medium, the greater prominence traditionally afforded arts specialists rather than drama specialists in schools, and greater interest in questions of seeing and perception within the visual arts.

Edmund Burke Feldman, a key writer in this field, sets out in *Varieties of Visual Experience* to

> give viewers a commonsense approach to the business of forming interpretations and making judgments about works of art. Although there are no permanently correct interpretations and evaluations of particular artworks, there are systematic procedures for going about the work of criticism. We should know what those procedures are and be able to use them. At least we should be able to defend the way we arrive at our opinions. (1992:467)

The alternative, says Feldman, is the current position where we all feel we have a democratic right to express our opinions on art. But these are typically instinctive; we parrot perspectives that have been foisted upon us by others or offer them without understanding where they come from.

Feldman describes the act of criticism as a kind of 'performance' which works best if it has order and sequence that allows us to make the best use of our knowledge, experience and powers of observation. Feldman's critical performance is laid out in four overlapping stages:

Description: Identifying what is there, ideally without inferences, judgements or personal responses.

Formal analysis: Exploring the relationships between the things we have named, considering how the component elements fit together – compositionally, thematically, physically, stylistically – to make a whole.

Interpretation: Finding meaning within what has been described and analysed.

Judgement: Articulating what we feel is the value or importance of a work of art, often in comparison with others.

Although intended for art viewers of all ages, adaptations based directly or indirectly upon Feldman's method and designed for schools and children are widely used in the United States (Taunton, 1983:40). Craig Roland, for example, has produced a model entitled 'Questions to ask kids about works of art'. This has a series of prompts under the following headings: describe it; relate it; analyse it; interpret it; evaluate it (Roland, 2007). The strength of the model is in the first instance precisely the order and system that Feldman demanded: by working through each of the stages, a viewer constructs, in sequence, a comprehensive critical response to a work of art that moves from observation and description through analysis and interpretation to evaluation. Each set of questions builds upon the answers of the last.

The model is also particularly appropriate for use with children, as it begins with questions that are easy to answer: what was it we just saw, heard, experienced? They are non-threatening and do not put anybody on the spot. Nonetheless, the observational and recognition skills required in what are sometimes termed 'lower order' memory or factual questions need careful and solid support, particularly in terms of responding to the multiple layers of a theatre performance and in terms of what to look at and how to describe it. The process of structuring a discussion in order to ask audiences to think about different aspects of a work in sequence and increasing complexity is useful when working with children.

In constructing an overall framework for an aesthetic enquiry, we also need to be aware of the importance of questioning techniques and the impact on classroom discussions of asking effective questions. Martha Taunton, for example, links the Feldman structural model to the need to be aware of the profound impact a teacher's response to a child's initial answer can have on the ensuing discussion. She suggests four 'probing' techniques seeking clarification; asking for justification of answers; refocusing the student's attention; providing prompts (1983:43). Good questioning techniques were discussed in Chapter Four and Ian Smith's *Asking Better Questions* (2007) is among the many good resources in this area.

The idea of organising questions through a framework that begins with appearances and surfaces, then moves on to more deductive reasoning and ends with aesthetic, evaluative or emotional responses to an art work has a commonsense logic to it. The four stages set out in the model – description, analysis, interpretation, judgement – essentially follow the four main stages of the critiquing process applied to any form of art, experience or process. Each element is vital and interdependent although, interestingly, within the history of art and literary criticism each has in turn been either strongly reviled or greatly celebrated. Description, for example, is celebrated by Susan Sontag in her essay 'Against Interpretation', where she demands art criticism that consists of 'accurate, sharp [and] loving description'. And she condemns interpretation as an act that serves 'to impoverish, to deplete the world – in order to set up a shadow world of 'meanings' (1967:7-12). Evaluation in criticism, meanwhile, is often condemned (not least by artists) as the meaningless assertion of one individual's opinion. Michael Kirby, for example, describes evaluative criticism as 'primitive and naïve, arrogant and immoral' (1974:66). Yet at the same time evaluation is so fundamental and instinctive that statements of personal opinion – I liked it; I loathed it – are central to our engagement with art.

A model of aesthetic enquiry which has some similarities with Feldman's systematic process of enquiry was developed by Project MUSE at the Harvard Graduate School of Education in the United States in 1994 to 1996. Led by Jessica Davis, Project MUSE was a collaboration between researchers, teachers, museum educators and schools to explore the potential to deepen the integration of art museums with education. A number of learning tools were developed, the most relevant of which is *The Generic Game*. In this activity a series of interconnected, open-ended questions are posed that do not have right or wrong answers. These are designed to be appropriate to young viewers of art without being too simplistic for expert viewers. The game was named 'generic' to signify its applicability and universality across a range of art works and art forms. Rather than needing particular knowledge or background or structure, the idea was that one set of questions would elicit responses built upon the others and 'scaffold' viewers' understanding of art from the outside details to more complex readings of a work of art (Davis, 2004:76-7).

All the models of aesthetic enquiry I have discussed emerged in the United States. One slightly different approach was originally developed in the UK by Catherine Orbach at Tate Liverpool. Designed to be used by schools and children engaging with visual materials, *Ways of Looking* is structured in four sections: 'A Personal Approach – What do I bring?'; 'Looking at the Subject: What is it about?'; 'Looking at the Object: What can I see?'; and finally 'Looking at the Context' (Charman and Ross, 2004). Elements of it can be traced directly to Feldman's model, with the section 'Looking at the object', for example, following a process of formally analysing the components of a work of art. It groups questions by various headings under which children might explore aspects of increasing complexity, including shapes, marks, surface, scale, space and colour.

What is striking about *Ways of Looking* is that it reverses the models described above by starting with a section entitled 'A Personal Approach: What do I bring?' it begins with the personal rather than the objective. Under the headings 'yourself', 'your world' and 'your experience', questions are presented that invite personal, interpretative and emotional responses to the work. A brief note explains that, 'all responses to works of art are conditioned by our different personal and social experiences. These cannot be ignored and should be our starting point when thinking about an artwork'. In articulating the objectives and effectiveness of this model, Helen Charman and Michaela Ross describe how this framework provides 'a loose but nonetheless methodological approach to looking at art':

> Each framework sets out a series of questions that give depth and breadth to the act of looking. The plural structures of interpretation offered by the four frameworks create plural outcomes, manifest as multiple interpretations of art works. (Charman and Ross, 2004)

While there is a richness and subtlety to the *Ways of Looking* framework, in losing some of the simplicity of the 'Describe, Analyse, Interpret, Evaluate' models, it also loses some of the immediacy, versatility and strength. What is required is something that allows the depth and breadth of the Tate model, but provides a more structured path in.

This brief survey outlines only the most significant of a range of models of aesthetic enquiry available in the visual arts. Thinking about my experience of using P4C in response to a theatre performance, I was intrigued as to what a model adapted for theatre might look like. I was particularly interested in how these models might be used to develop a generic resource for post-performance discussions that could be used to elicit open, reflective and self-interrogative responses to any theatre performance. But I thought the tradition within theatre studies of semiotic analysis might offer an alternative.

Semiotics and theatre studies

Semiotics is the study of signs: of how meaning is constructed and communicated through our creation and interpretation of signs. Signs can take the form of words, images, sounds, odours, flavours, acts or objects that someone interprets as signifying something, as referring to or standing for something other than itself. So, for example, a red rose may be a flower but it also has connotations of love, England, Lancashire, Valentine's Day, Mills and Boon, the film *American Beauty*, the English rugby team, the Labour party and so on. While, as Gertrude Stein asserted, a rose is a rose is a rose, it is potentially connotive of any number of things according to how we interpret it and our own cultural experiences. We interpret things as signs largely unconsciously by relating them to learnt systems and conventions. It is this meaningful use of signs that is at the heart of semiotics.

The ways and levels on which signs work is complex and not a subject I want to develop here. But it provides a structure of analysis that has become prominent in cultural studies, literature and art criticism and, not least, in theatre studies. Elaine Aston and George Savona, for example, describe how theatre semiotics is 'a *methodology*: a way of working, of approaching theatre in order to open up new practices and possibilities of 'seeing'' (1991:1).

One of the most significant projects of theatre semiotics has been the attempt to map out sign-systems as they appear in performance. Once framed, by being placed on a stage for example, everything has a signifying function. Moreover, once framed, the semiotic function of anything supersedes its normal function in the everyday world. As Keir Elam writes:

> The stage radically transforms all objects and bodies defined within it, bestowing upon them an overriding signifying power which they lack – or which at least is less evident – in their normal social function. (1980:7)

So, to pursue our example, if we see a rose in a front garden it might cause us to respond in various ways but the flower is not taken as explicitly meaningful. If we see the same thing on a stage, however, we can be certain that it has intention and meaning that we must seek out and interpret. In criticism, therefore, the convention is to perceive everything present within the performance as being there for a reason – it has a function, a purpose, meaning; it has been deliberately chosen and presented to us. A chair on stage is not any random chair, but that particular chair, and that particular chair has a particular meaning. Think of the difference between a throne, a rocking chair, a plastic school chair, an armchair...

If everything on stage is a sign – and that means *everything* – then theatre studies needs a method analysis that can systematically account for everything – text, tone, gesture, movement, make-up, costumes, props, lighting, music, sets and so forth. We must ask why that chair? Why that colour? Why that music? Audiences intuitively begin the process of what is labelled semiotic analysis without having to know any of the theory. Moreover, as Ubersfeld suggests, the process of seeing and interpreting signs is the fundamental pleasure of theatre (1982:129).

Various taxonomies of classification have been developed to enable semiotic analysis of this kind, mostly aimed at university students. In the 1960, Tadeusz Kowzan provided a classification with thirteen categories of signs, while Martin Esslin increased this to twenty-two (Aston and Savona, 1991:108). The most significant and enduring work in this area is the Pavis Questionnaire, a series of questions grouped under headings (Scenography, Costume, the Actors' Performance, Audience etc).

The Pavis Questionnaire has many valuable elements, including accessibility. It was designed for use by students who had no background in semiotics, and its 'listing of the aesthetic problems enable the questionnaire to be used as a checklist (even an 'idiot's guide') for the study of performance' (Pavis, 1985: 208-12). Implicit within the structure of the questions, it has the same movement from description to analysis that Edmund Feldman described in his structure of criticism. According to Aston and Savona:

> It usefulness lies in its listing of theatrical sign-systems, the basic 'what to look for' approach, but it also guides the student from identification to an analysis of signification by virtue of the sub-questioning/discussion points offered within the categories. It constantly addresses the question of 'how' meaning is constructed and creates the possibility of guiding the student from the 'how' to the 'why'. (1991:109)

This movement – from what, to how, to why – is not a matter of increasing complexity but of careful layering, each layer built upon the answers that came before. The Pavis Questionnaire is designed for adult or near adult students of theatre. However, while the terminology and theory of semiotics is clearly not of interest to young children, the act of what we might term semiotic analysis – the reading of meaning from signs – is not beyond their grasp. We saw in Chapter Six, for example, how children were able to transform various visual and audio signifiers – sound effects of people playing on the beach, the noise of seagulls, characters wearing sunglasses, the hanging up of washing – and translate this into an overall referent of sunny-day-ness. So I became interested in the possibility of developing a method of aesthetic enquiry for theatre which children could use, which drew on not just the Pavis Questionnaire but also the models existing within the visual arts.

The 'Talking about Theatre' model

Having explored the various models and processes described above – P4C, methods of aesthetic enquiry within visual arts and semiotic analysis in theatre studies and the Pavis Questionnaire – I sought to develop a model of aesthetic enquiry that could be used by children and teachers in response to a theatre performance. This was conducted in collaboration with Imaginate and through consultation with their teachers' advisor group. The objective is to provide a structure that enhances discussion, rather than a prison that limits it. As Taunton writes:

> a lively classroom dialogue about art uses the process of art criticism as a guide, but it also will achieve an existence of its own due to the children and the teacher involved. (1983:42)

Many of the guiding principles for this project encapsulate points made in this chapter:

Children as critics

Responding to and talking about art experience is a social need and it is vital to the experience itself. There is pleasure in understanding that enhances the experience and empowers the audience. So we should aim to provide children and young people with a structure in which they can develop their abilities as reflective and analytical critics.

Describe, analyse, interpret, evaluate

The model should follow the systematic process of developing the analysis through stages that build upon each other. Each stage in this is vital, including the right of children to their personal responses and opinions. The objective is not to change minds but to increase skills of observation, analysis, reflection and articulation. Criticism is something we do, a practical activity in which we can develop our ability.

Semiotic analysis

Children already respond to performances on sophisticated levels that indicate their unconscious reading of theatrical signs and conventions. The careful articulation of the elements of the whole, how they work together, what they mean, how they construct meaning, are all central to semiotic analysis and are potentially within the grasp of children responding to a production.

An aesthetic enquiry

The process should be open and accessible, with different access points for different age groups. The objective was a model that was generic: while some aspects might be more relevant to some performances than others, unlike many post-performance resources our process would not be specific to a particular production but would be a form of open aesthetic enquiry that could be applied to any theatre experience.

The role of the teacher

The model should provide a process that requires facilitation but not instruction by an expert who has all the answers. When used in schools this would shift the role of the teacher from instructor to a role more like the one required in Philosophy for Children. Although in some sense a challenge for teachers, being repositioned as someone who is not expected to know everything is liberating. After a performance children often bombard their teacher with questions, to which they might not know the answers or feel confident about, whereas the model of Talking about Theatre requires the children to ask questions of each other and themselves.

Talking about Theatre is an integral part of the theatrical encounter and it deepens and extends the original experience. Engaging in dialogue, asking questions and recalling observation are skills – abilities that need to be fostered, taught and encouraged. The model presented below provides one approach through which this might take place. Talking about theatre should above all be part of the pleasure of theatre.

Talking *about* Theatre

Produced by Matthew Reason (York St John University) in collaboration with Imaginate

The post-show conversation and discussion is fundamental to the experience of theatre. We have a powerful need to talk about the production, to share memories, interpretations and experiences. While talking about theatre after the event may be instinctive, such conversation benefits from being supported through a structure and set of questions designed to encourage participation, deepen thinking and sharpen insights.

Making time to reflect on the experience after attending a theatre performance can extend pupils' overall experience and develop their critical thinking skills. It will also answer the many questions they may have. Critical discussions about art provide us with pleasure, through understanding and reflection, and enable us to become better and more active audience members.

The role and craft of asking good questions has long been recognised as a vital part of teaching and learning, with the structure and sample questions presented here providing a framework for initiating and sustaining dialogue about a theatre performance. Using this structure to guide the process of talking – and thinking – about theatre, will ensure that conversation goes beyond recall and surface evaluation (did you enjoy it?) and begins to tackle the theatrical experience in depth and detail.

Using this resource

The role and value of encouraging children and young people to develop skills in *understanding, analysing* and *evaluating* texts of all forms, including theatre and other art works, is recognised as a cross-curricula responsibility. The experience of theatre and the other expressive arts provides opportunities to develop the knowledge, understanding and appreciation children and young people have of contemporary and historical arts within their own communities, nationally and beyond. And engaging with the arts as active and analytical audience members encourages empathy and cognitive abilities.

The outcomes across all curriculum levels encourage children and young people to discuss their *thoughts* and *feelings* in response to art with the objective of developing the ability of making *informed judgement* and *considered opinions*. Talking about Theatre is designed to support teachers in finding ways of sustaining discussion about performing arts experiences with pupils, supporting them in making informed value judgements and developing skills in art criticism.

An infinite range of conversations could be had about theatre, depending on the form, style and content of the performance and the learning styles and age of the audience. Talking about Theatre provides a structure for organising an enquiry into almost any theatre experience. It is designed to support a process whereby pupils can learn to provide reasons for preferences. Learning how to respond critically to artworks allows pupils to better understand works of art while at the same time being able to express their own personal opinion. To do this it adopts a model of art criticism involving four actions – *description, analysis, interpretation* and *evaluation*. Working through the whole resource could run over an hour of discussion; you may wish to spread this over a few days, providing thinking time in between stages.

Activity	Useful questions	Discussion / Learning Opportunities
First impressions *Likes and dislikes.*	**What did you think of it?** Often the first thing we do when leaving the theatre is turn to our neighbour and ask 'Well, what did you think?' This is a vital first stage of responses to art and might take place informally – on the bus on the way home, for example – and possibly without an adult being aware of the conversation. If you want to conduct this stage more formally you might want to gather first impressions through 'pair and share', which will ensure that everybody gets a chance to make some input. One idea would be to ask pupils to record their initial responses and return to these at the end of the discussion.	It is always a good starting place to learn about others' personal thoughts and feelings about a performance. Liking and disliking are fundamental to our responses to art, and such evaluative judgements are a central part of art criticism. This activity allows space for these immediate and unrefined responses.

Activity	Useful questions	Discussion / Learning Opportunities
DESCRIPTION *What was it we just saw?*	Sit in a circle with the group and start to explore memories of the performance. Begin by asking: **Tell us something you remember from the performance.** **What did you see / feel / hear / smell?** Encourage each student to think of their own memory or a different one from what has already been mentioned. Everyone in the group should take a turn sharing a memory of the performance, no matter how small. Proceed round a circle, perhaps more than once. It is useful to write the memories down on the white-board, on large pieces of paper or as notes as you will come back to them later. Expanding the discussion: If the answers are very short (such as simply 'the set') you may want to encourage individuals to expand on their perceptions by using open questions and encouragement, such as: **Could you tell us more about that?**	A lot can happen in a theatre performance and when we come to discuss it afterwards it has often already begun to disappear into our memory. It is therefore useful to begin with a process of memory retrieval, collecting and sharing experiences, gathering descriptions of what was seen and heard. Gathered collectively from a group, these descriptions will begin to construct a rich, detailed description of the performance. This rich description is the first stage of art criticism.

Activity	Useful questions	Discussion / Learning Opportunities
ANALYSIS *How do the different elements of the production fit together?*	As pupils present memories the next step is to order them and identify what different aspects were doing in the production: *What* was seen/heard? *How* did they impact on the experience? Group their responses in categories, using the sample questions on the prompt cards on page 163-166. Encourage your pupils to think about them in relation to specific aspects of the performance. Each prompt card asks questions about the following aspects of the production: • Set • Props • Lighting • Costume • Actors and Characters • Music • Sound • Speech and Language • The Audience • Direction If your class is new to theatre you might want to introduce and discuss each of these terms before giving them the prompt cards.	In art criticism the convention is to perceive everything present within the performance as being there for a reason. Everything has been deliberately chosen and presented to us and becomes a sign with meaning and purpose beyond its simple presence. Part of the audience's task is to interpret these signs, thinking about *what* they are doing there; why they are chosen; and *how* this affects our experience. Doing this will support pupils in understanding how art communicates.

Activity	Useful questions
ANALYSIS (continued)	We suggest you divide the class into small groups or pairs looking at one category each, recording their discussion on paper or notes, then ask each group to present their findings or carousel around the groups.
	You'll notice that each prompt card ends with a question asking:
	What did the set/lighting/costumes etc tell you about...
	This question asks pupils to think about *how* and *why* the different aspects of the performance were put together and consider why the director made the particular choices they did.
	Prompting further discussion:
	If pupils are struggling to respond, an interesting option is to ask what they might have done differently if they had been the director. This requires pupils to think about the reasons behind their choices and the impact they have.

159

Activity	Useful questions	Discussion / Learning Opportunities
INTERPRETATION *What did it mean to me?*	Interpretation is the process of finding meaning within what has been described and analysed. This must not be a deadening process and it might not necessarily result in answers everybody agrees upon. The following questions are designed to initiate more creative, speculative and yet still interpretative conversation about the performance. Some are intentionally surprising or playful. They may need to be adapted according to the performance and the children's age and experience. **You can choose to ask just one question or many:** • What different title could you give to the performance? And why? • If the performance had lasted longer, what else might have happened? How would this have changed its meaning?	Interpretative discussion is about open questions of what an artwork means to us and how and why it means that. In art criticism the critic's interpretations form a kind of bridge between an art work and its audience. You don't need to be a professional art critic to make interpretations, and these exercises allow pupils to engage with the performance as an expressive form and articulate its impact and meaning for them. *Cross-curricular work* Interpretation can also occur when we seek to transform our experience into another form. You might ask pupils to produce a drawing, poem/haiku, model, script, newspaper report, diary or performance (such as freeze frame a key moment for each character) that responds to one of the questions suggested here.

Activity	Useful questions
INTERPRETATION (continued)	• Did the performance make you think or feel anything about your own life? Can you tell us how and why? • If the performance was a noise or a colour, what would it be? And why? • If you could be one of the characters in the performance, which one would it be and why? • What would you have changed about the performance? Why? We think these questions are best answered as an individual activity, perhaps working in thinking books or another method that allows thinking time before responding. You might want to set a question for children to think about and come back to the following day. _And why?_ The supplementary explanation required above – and _why?_ – are obviously vital. Use open prompts to encourage greater responses here: Why do you think that? Can you explain what you mean by...? What evidence do you have for that...?

Activity	Useful questions	Discussion / Learning Opportunities
EVALUATION *Expression of reasoned opinions.*	Evaluation looks at why you like or dislike the performance. After considering all the aspects above base your opinions on considered judgement as well as personal opinion. The individual activity of interpretation should be followed with a final group discussion around some of the following questions: • Has anybody changed their minds about the performance following our discussion? • Who would you recommend should or should not see this performance? • What do you think you'll remember about the performance in the future?	Returning to the same theme with which the discussion began – did you like the performance? – recognises that the evaluative response of like or dislike is vital. It recognises that even after the discussion individuals might have different tastes and affirms pupils' right to their own opinions. The objective is not to change minds, although if that happens it is interesting to explore why. Hopefully, however, preferences will now be more readily supported with explanations and reasons.

Analysing the Performance: Some Useful Questions

Each box here asks a set of questions in relation to different aspects of the production:

- Set
- Lighting
- Actors and Characters
- Sound
- The Audience
- Props
- Costume
- Music
- Speech and Language
- Direction

Divide these questions among the class as prompt cards, to assist small groups or pairs to think about each category. Ask each group to present their findings or carousel around the groups.

The questions are generic and may be more or less relevant to different productions. Feel free to add or make up your own.

Set

Did the set look like something from real life? In what ways?

Was the set contemporary or historical? In what ways?

How did the set change during the production?

Did anything look out of place or odd?

What shapes or objects were there in the set?

What colours were there in the set? Which were strongest or most important?

What was up high? What was low down?

What did the set tell you about the location of the production; or about its mood/atmosphere?

Costume

Were the actors wearing costumes or everyday clothes?

What shapes or textures were there in the costumes?

What colours were there in the costumes? Which were strongest or most important?

What impact did the costumes have on how the actors moved or talked?

Did the costumes help you identify the characters or indicate anything about their personality?

What did the costumes tell you about the time or place; or about the characters; or about the mood of the production?

Props	Music	Sound
What props – things, objects of any sort – were there in the production?	What different kinds of music were used in the performance?	What non-musical sounds were there in the production?
Did any of these look out of place or odd? In what ways?	Was the music played by the actors or did it come from offstage? Was the music part of the story or incidental/atmospheric?	Were these sounds made by the performers on stage or did they come from off stage?
Did any props have more than one function? Were they used in different ways?	How did the music affect the mood of the production?	Were these sounds realistic? In what ways?
How did the props relate to characters? In what ways? Did they impact on the actors' movements?	Was music matched to particular characters?	**What did the sounds tell you about the time, place or mood of the performance?**
Did any of the props have symbolic importance?	**What did the music tell you about the mood of the production; about the story; about the time and place?**	
What did the props tell you about the setting of the production or about the characters?	**What did the music tell you about the characters?**	

Lighting

How would you describe the lighting? Was it bright, dark, spotlights, coloured, everyday or special?

How did the lighting change during the production?

How did the lighting affect the mood of the production?

Was lighting used to divide up the space? To create illusions of things that weren't there? To create shapes?

What did the lighting tell you about the time of day; or about the location; or about the mood of the production?

Speech and Language

Do you think the actors were speaking lines they had learnt or making it up as they went along? Did they ever improvise?

Was there an off-stage voiceover? If so, whose was this voice?

Did the speech have a particular accent? What different volumes did it have? What different tones (emotions) did it have?

Were there any memorable lines?

What did the speech and language tell you about the time or place of the production or about the characters?

Audience

Where did the performance take place? Was this a formal or informal context? How did this impact on the experience?

What was the target audience for the production? What expectations did it provoke?

How did the audience respond to the performance?

Was everything made clear to the audience or was anything left unclear?

What impact did watching in an audience have on the production and what impact might the production have had on the audience?

Actors and Characters

Did the performers appear as themselves or as characters? How did you know?

What different characters were there?

Could you describe their personalities? How did you know this was their personality?

In what particular ways did the characters move or gesture? Could you describe how they walked, or smiled, or laughed? What effect did this have?

What was the physical appearance of the actors? Was this affected by their speech or costumes?

Did the characters speak to you (the audience) directly or only to each other?

What did the acting and characters tell you about the setting; or about the mood; or about the moral/message of the production?

Story or Meaning

If there was a narrative, could you summarise it?

Was the story told in a linear or circular manner? What was the impact of this?

What were the crucial turning points in the story?

What was the genre of the story?

Did the production have an underlying meaning (moral, message, theme)? How was this communicated?

Were the story and/or meaning true to life and believable?

What was the impact of the narrative on your experience of the production?

Direction

What was the overall pace of the production?

Were there any elements that were slower or faster? If so, why?

Did all the elements of the production (set, lighting, costume, acting etc) work together? Why/why not?

Were there any deliberate inconsistencies?

Was there anything surprising about the production? If so, what?

What were the dominant elements which held the production together?

Did the production have a unified style, genre, appearance?

What did the direction suggest was most important in the production?

Conclusion
The Audience's Gaze

'Looking'
Photographs by Lisa Barnard
Originally commissioned for the Unicorn Theatre as part of a photographic residency
supported by Pool of London Partnerships and Arts Council South East

Conclusion
The Audience's Gaze

In a book about how children watch theatre it is appropriate to include Lisa Barnard's striking photographs of children watching a performance at the Unicorn Theatre in London. Theatre is made to be experienced and Barnard's photographs allow us to reflect upon the act of looking.

The act of watching theatre is at once very public and yet also very private. It is public in that it takes place in a public place; indeed, theatre is often described as being a communal form and about shared experiences. But watching is also private, an activity that takes place through the eyes and in the mind and which – except at certain moments – is not necessarily made manifest upon the face. Looking at the children in Barnard's photographs, we cannot know exactly what they are thinking or what they are seeing or how they are responding, although all of this concealment is taking place in public. In seeking to explore how children experience theatre, the challenge for this book has been precisely to try to discover something of the private experience of a public event.

It is vital, however, that we take up the challenge if we want to know what young audiences make of their theatrical experiences. And if we are not interested in how children engage with theatre, then how seriously are we taking our audience in the theatre that we make *for* them? The implications of the preposition *for* are interesting and worth dwelling on.

Children in our society are largely constructed as powerless: as vulnerable, dependent, needing protection and needing to be spoken for. With theatre for children this powerlessness is manifested in the preposition for. For children, but by the adult author, artist, director, actor. And also for children in being for their good, their benefit, their education.

It is the power imbalance between adults and children maintained within this preposition that leads Jacqueline Rose to assert the 'impossibility' of fiction for children (1984). And that leads Stephen Klein to write that 'what might be taken as children's culture has always been primarily a matter of culture produced for and urged upon children'. Klein suggests that the notion of culture for children requires a silenced child whose voice is assumed by adults; a muteness that largely equates to powerlessness over those cultural experiences (1998:95).

The concept of theatre *for* children situates children as the audience, which can be perceived as a largely passive and disempowered position: watchers rather than actors; observers rather than participants; spoken to, rather than speaking. The theatre audience is, literally and typically, required to be silent, only heard at appropriate moments. This perception of the audience as there to be entertained, doing little else but sitting still, is most familiar to us in the slouch-backed, coach-potato imagery of passive consumption associated with television or video games. It might be argued, however, that the theatre audience is just as inactive and submissive – part of a wider cultural concern that watching is replacing doing; seeing replacing experiencing.

Barnard's pictures of children watching theatre have some of these qualities. The expressions are not blank, but there is a closed quality to the children's faces, which are bathed in a glow that in its effect is not unlike that of the mesmerising television screen. The stillness in the faces, the distant raptness of the expressions and the almost glazed quality of the eyes may lead us to believe that the audience's experience of theatre is largely passive.

However, while the transfixed eye might suggest passivity, it might alterna- tively be take as a supreme level of engagement. Children are frequently described as the most honest of audiences. If a production is poor or un- interesting they will fidget and shuffle, talk and look away. If, on the other hand, a production is gripping they can be still and transfixed – more so even than adults. And the transfixed audience is one that may be passive externally (publicly) but internally (privately) is very active – at work in interpreting, engaging, analysing and constructing what is going on in front of them.

While the public face and outward visage of the audience might be passive – the result of a cultural contract wherein the audience agrees to sit still, watch and listen – the private and inward experience of an engaged audience is any- thing but. The dual conception of the audience – outwardly passive, inwardly active – is strongly asserted within theatre studies and audience research. Susan Bennett, for example, writes that 'spectators are trained to be passive in their demonstrated behaviour during a theatrical performance, but to be active in their decoding of the sign systems made available' (1997:206). Or, as

Ubersfeld writes, 'theatrical pleasures are rarely passive; 'doing' plays a larger role than 'receiving'' (1982:132).

The 'doing' of the audience is multiple, the doing of pleasures and engagements and processes with which spectators respond to performances as they watch and after the event. The doing of the audience has been the primary focus of this book as it has sought to describe and analyse how children watch theatre. It has examined the dual vision by which young audiences engage with the evoked experience of illusion, narrative and character and at the same time with the material appearance of staging, technique and performance. This dual vision involves the active reading across from one element of the experience to the other, with engagement with the craft and material reality of the production enhancing engagement with the illusion evoked.

We noted young audiences' active engagement with theatre and their theatrical competences and ability not only to interpret the signs and conventions of theatre but also to reflect back upon and articulate their own interpretation. The reward of watching theatre was often found in the act itself and in active and reflective engagement with the experience. This pleasure of understanding and knowledge is active, not passive.

The young audiences I worked with exhibited pleasure in their post-performance engagement with the performances. They enjoyed remembering, discussing and making art works in response to the performances in the research workshops afterwards. The post-performance workshops actively enhanced the experience for the children, providing a structure through which their engagement with the performance could endure and resonate. Talking about, (mis)remembering the performance and transforming the experience into drawings and other art works required the children to be active spectators and think back over the experience, internalise it, embellish it, transform it and, as a result, begin to own the experience for themselves. The adult author, artist, director or artist loses control and the performance and meaning of the experience becomes the property of the audience.

The way children use, play with and transform their cultural experiences in their imaginative lives reveals how the passive consumer is in reality an active participant. Acquiring knowledge, and skills of reflection and criticality, enables the powerless child to become enfranchised and empowered by their own cultural experiences. That is why the relationship between young audiences and theatre should never be conceptualised merely in terms of access, of getting bums on seats and of cultural rights equating simply to exposure to rich cultural experiences. Cultural rights must encompass art form knowledge and criticality as essential elements in the empowerment of young audiences.

Look again at Barnard's photographs and think about what might be going on behind the transfixed gaze. Think of this in terms of the active processes of decoding and responding that take place during the performance; and the ways in which the experience might resonate and endure in the children's own cultural and imaginative lives after the performance.

We should also think about the transfixed eye itself, described within critical theory as the gaze and discussed in terms of scopophilia or the pleasure of looking and often in terms of its erotic, voyeuristic and unsettling functions. Children are often told to stop staring: adults find it unsettling and such stares have the power to move. As Herbert Blau writes, 'there is in the transfixed eyeball a reflection of a coercive power' (1990:6). In the theatre each individual's attention is focused on the performance; nobody is looking at the audience. The children in Barnard's images look unguarded; they do not expect to be observed. The audience is given licence to look searchingly at the stage and the people upon it in a way that would be taboo in everyday life. The force of this collectively transfixed gaze is something performers report to be tangible; through it the actor can feel the audience.

This pleasure of looking, of staring and wonderment, combines with the other pleasures of the spectator described in this book: the conscious and reflective pleasures that come from knowledge and understanding; the emotional pleasures that come from empathy and wonderment; and the social pleasures that come from shared experiences. Whether we think of staring or gazing or watching or witnessing, what we are dealing with is audiencing. Theatre is made to be experienced and consideration of the nature of that experience needs to be fully understood. In this book I have tried to explore how spectatorship can be conceived as an active doing and not a passive lack of doing.

I hope this book will invigorate and empower those who engage with children and theatre, be they parents, teachers, artists or education workers. I hope I have provided the insights, knowledge and tools that will allow us all to become active researchers into children's experiences of theatre and facilitate children in becoming empowered and self-reflective audience members. This way we will learn more about both children's and our own experiences of theatre and thereby enrich our engagement with the art form and make it resonate for longer.

References

Adams, Eileen (2002) Power Drawing. *International Journal of Art and Design Education*, 21 (3) 220-233

Adams, Eileen and Baynes, Ken (2003) *Power Drawing Notebooks,* London, Drawing Power, The Campaign for Drawing

Anning, Angela and Ring, Kathy (2004) *Making Sense of Children's Drawings*, Maidenhead, Open University Press

Ariès, Philippe (1979) *Centuries of Childhood,* Hammondsworth, Penguin

Arnold, Andy (2005) *An Arches View on the Way Forward...* Public Submission to the Cultural Commission. Available: www.culturalcommission.org

Asthana, Anushka and Thorpe, Vanessa (2007) Arts Chief Warns of Cultural 'Apartheid'. *The Observer.* 2 December, London

Aston, Elaine and Savona, George (1991) *Theatre as Sign-System: A semiotics of text and performance*, London, Routledge

Barba, Eugenio (1992) Efermaele: 'That which will be said afterwards'. *The Drama Review*, 36 (2) 77-80

Bennett, Stuart (2005) Introduction: A history and perspective. In Bennett, S (ed) *Theatre for Children and Young People: 50 years of professional theatre in the UK.* London, Aurora Metro Press

Bennett, Susan (1997) *Theatre Audiences: A theory of production and reception,* London, Routledge

Blau, Herbert (1990) *The Audience*, Baltimore, John Hopkins University Press.

Bogatyrev, Petr (1983) The Interconnection of Two similar Semiotic Systems: The puppet theatre and the theatre of living actors. *Semiotica*, 47 (1/4) 47-68

Boon, Jain (2005) Children's Theatre and Emotional Literacy. In Bennett, S (ed) *Theatre for Children and Young People*. London, Aurora Metro Press

Bourdieu, Pierre (1984) *Distinction: A social critique of the judgement of taste*, London, Routledge and Kegan Paul

Bresler, Liora and Thompson, Christine Marme (eds) (2002) *The Art in Children's Lives: Context, culture and curriculum*, Dordrecht, NL, Kluwer Academic Publishers

Brosius, Peter C. (2001) Can Theater + Young People = Social Change? The Answer Must Be Yes. *Theater*, 31 (3) 74-75

Burnard, Pamela (2000) How Children Ascribe Meaning to Improvisation and Composition. *Music Education Research*, 2 (1) 7-23

Burton, Judith, Horowitz, Robert and Abeles, Hal (1999) Learning Through the Arts: Curriculum implications. In Fiske, EB (ed) *Champions of Change: The impact of the arts on learning.* Washington DC, Arts Education Partnership

Catterall, James S, Chapleau, Richard and Iwanaga, John (1999) Involvement in the Arts and Human Development: General involvement and intensive involvement in music and theatre arts. In Fiske, EB (ed) *Champions of Change: The impact of the arts on learning.* Washington DC, Arts Education Partnership

Cazeaux, Clive (ed) (2000) *The Continental Aesthetics Reader*, Abingdon, Routledge

Charman, Helen and Ross, Michaela (2004) *Contemporary Art and the Role of Interpretation.* Tate Papers. Available: www.tate.org.uk/research/tateresearch/tatepapers/04autumn/charman.htm

Christensen, Pia and James, Allison (eds) (2000) *Research with Children: Perspectives and practices,* London, Falmer Press

Clark, Anthony (2002) *The Quality of Children's Theatre.* Birmingham, Arts Council of England

Clifford, John (2000) *Hansel and Gretel* and the Art of Children's Theatre. *Edinburgh Review,* 105, 65-72

Coates, Elizabeth (2004) 'I Forgot the Sky!' Children's stories contained within their drawings. In Lewis, V, Kellett, M, Robinson, C, Fraser, S and Ding, S (eds) *The Reality of Research with Children and Young People.* London, Sage/OUP

Cultural Commission (2005) *Final Report of the Cultural Commission.* Edinburgh, Scottish Executive. Available: www.culturalcommission.org

Davis, Jessica (2004) *The Muse Book: A report on the work of Project Muse.* Cambridge, MA, Harvard Graduate School of Education

Dewey, John (1934) *Art as Experience,* New York, Minton, Blach and Co

Donders, Yvonne (2004) The Legal Framework of the Right to Take Part in Cultural Life. Conference on Cultural Rights and Human Development. Barcelona. Available: www.culturalrights.org

Downing, Dick, Ashworth, Mary and Scott, Alison (2002) *Acting with Intent: Theatre companies and their education programmes.* Slough, National Foundation for Education Research

Downing, Dick, Johnson, Fiona and Kaur, Satpal (2003) *Saving a Place for the Arts? A survey of the arts in primary schools in England.* Slough, NFER

Drury, Martin (2006) Steering the Ark: A cultural centre for children. *Teaching Artist Journal,* 4 (3) 149-157

Elam, Keir (1980) *The Semiotics of Theatre and Drama,* London, Methuen

Feldman, Edmund Burke (1992) *Varities of Visual Experiences,* New York, H.N. Abrams

Fiske, Edward B (ed) (1999) *Champions of Change: The impact of the arts on learning,* Washington, DC, The Arts Education Partnership

Ford, Michelle and Wooder, Dot (1997) *Is it in Colour, Miss? The first fifty years of the Unicorn Theatre for Children,* London, Unicorn Theatre

Freshwater, Helen (2009) *Theatre and Audience,* Houndmills, Palgrave Macmillan.

Gardner, Lyn (2002) *The Quality of Children's Theatre.* Birmingham, Arts Council of England

Gauntlett, David (2004) *Using New Creative Visual Research Methods to Understand the Place of Popular Media in People's Lives.* IAMCR

Geraghty, Christine (1998) Audiences and 'Ethnography': Questions of practice. In Geraghty, C and Lusted, D (eds) *The Television Studies Book.* London, Arnold 141-157

Goldberg, Moses (1974) *Children's Theatre: A philosophy and a method,* New Jersey, Prentice Hall

Graham, Tony (2005) Unicorn: The pioneer children's theatre. In Bennett, S (ed) *Theatre for Children and Young People.* Aurora Metro Press

Greene, Sheila and Hill, Malcolm (2005) Researching Children's Experiences: Methods and methodological issues. In Greene, S and Hogan, D (eds) *Researching Children's Experiences.* London, Sage

Guenther, Katja M (2009) The politics of names: rethinking the methodological and ethical significance of naming people, organisations and places. *Qualitative Research* 9(4) 411-421

Harland, John, Kinder, Kay and Hartley, Kate (1995) *Arts in Their View: A study of youth participation in the arts*, Slough, National Foundation for Educational Research

Harland, John, Kinder, Kay, Lord, Pippa, Stott, Alison, Schagen, Ian and Haynes, Jo (2000) *Arts Education in Secondary Schools: Effects and effectiveness*, Slough, National Federation for Education Research

Haynes, Joanna (2002) *Children as Philosophers*, London, Routledge Falmer

Heron, John (1996) *Co-operative Inquiry: Research into the human condition*, London, Sage

Holland, Norman (1981) Criticism as Transaction. In Hernadi, P (ed) *What is Criticism?* Bloomington, Indiana University Press

Hood, Suzanne, Kelley, Peter and Mayall, Berry (1996) Children as Research Subjects: A risky enterprise. *Children and Society*, 10 (2) 117-128

Jackson, Tony (1993) Introduction. In Jackson, T (ed) *Learning Through Theatre: New perspectives on Theatre in Education*. London, Routledge

Jowitt, Deborah (1977) *Dance Beat: Selected views and reviews 1967-1976*, New York, Marcel Dekker

Jurkowski, Henryk (1983) Transcodification of the Sign Systems of Puppetry. *Semiotics*, 47 (1-4) 123-146

Kirby, Michael (1974) Criticism: Four Faults. *The Drama Review*, 18 (3) 59-68

Klein, Jeanne (1987) Children's Processing of Theatre as a Function of Verbal and Visual Recall. *Youth Theatre Journal*, 2 (1) 9-13

Klein, Jeanne (1989) Third Grade Children's Verbal and Visual Recall of Monkey, Monkey. *Youth Theatre Journal*, 4 (2) 9-15

Klein, Jeanne (1990) First Grade Children's Comprehension of Noodle Doodle Box. *Youth Theatre Journal*, 5 (2) 7-13

Klein, Jeanne (1993) Applying Research to Artistic Practices: This is not a pipe dream. *Youth Theatre Journal*, 7 (3) 13-17

Klein, Jeanne (2005) From Children's Perspective: A model of aesthetic processing in theatre. *Journal of Aesthetic Education*, 39 (4) 40-57

Klein, Stephen (1998) The Making of Children's Culture. In Jenkins, H (ed) *The Children's Culture Reader*. New York, New York University

Laaksonen, Annamari (2005) *Measuring Exclusion Through Participation in Cultural Life*. Third Global Forum on Human Development. Paris

Liptai, Sara (2004) *Two Pictures and Two Pieces of Music: How are they connected?* ECME. Barcelona

Liptai, Sara (2005) What is the Meaning of this Cup and that Dead Shark? Philosophical inquiry with objects and works of art and craft. *Childhood and Philosophy*, 1(2). Available: www.filoeduc. org/childphilo/n2/SaraLiptai.htm

Lutley, Phyllis & Demmery, Sylvia (1978) *Theatre for Children and Theatre in Education*, Bromley, Educational Drama Association

Malchiodi, Cathy A (1998) *Understanding Children's Drawings*, London, Jessica Kingsley

Matthews, Gareth B (1980) *Philosophy and the Young Child*, Cambridge, Mass, Harvard University Press

Matthews, John (1999) *The Art of Childhood and Adolescence: The construction of meaning*, London, Falmer Press

Mayall, Berry (2000) Conversations with Children: Working with generational issues. In Christensen, P and James, A (eds) *Research with Children: Perspectives and practices*. London, Falmer

McMaster, Brian (2008) *Supporting Excellence in the Arts: From measurement to judgement*. London, Department for culture, media and sport

McNaughton, Marie Jeanne, Mitchell, Liz and Eaton, Wilma (2003) *A Curriculum for Excellence, Review of Research Literature: Expressive Arts*. Glasgow, University of Strathclyde

Melzer, Annabelle (1995) 'Best Betrayal': The documentation of performance on film and video, part 1. *New Theatre Quarterly,* 11 (42) 147-157

Morag Ballantyne Arts Management (2001) *Education and Audience Development Audit*. Edinburgh, Scottish Arts Council

Morrison, David E (1998) *The Search for a Method: Focus groups and the development of mass communication research*, Luton, University of Luton Press

Morrison, William G and West, Edwin G (1986) Child Exposure to the Performing Arts: The implications for adult demand. *Journal of Cultural Economics,* 10 (1) 17-24

Morrow, Virginia and Richards, Martin (1996) The Ethics of Social Research with Children: An overview. *Children and Society,* 10 (2) 90-105

National Endowment for the Arts (1992) *Effects of Arts Education on Participation in the Arts*. Washington DC: National Endowment for the Arts

Naysmith, Stephen (2005) Is it curtains for school theatre trips? *The Herald* 28 June. Glasgow

NFO System Three (2002) *Attendance at, Participation in and Attitudes towards the Arts in Scotland*. Edinburgh, Scottish Arts Council

O'Brien, Jane (1996) *Secondary School Pupils and the Arts: Report of a MORI Research Study*. London, Arts Council of England

O'Neill, Cecily (2005) I*magination in Action: Unicorn Education 1997-2005*. London, Unicorn Theatre

Pavis, Patrice (1985) Theatre Analysis: Some questions and a questionnaire. *New Theatre Quarterly,* 1 (2) 208-12

Pipe, Margaret-Ellen, Salmon, Karen and Preistley, Gina K (2002) Enhancing Children's Accounts: How useful are non-verbal techniques. In Westcott, H L, Davies, G M and Bull, R H (eds) *Children's Testimony: A Handbook of Psychological Research and Forensic Practice*. Chichester, Wiley

Pullman, Philip (2004) Theatre – the true key stage. *The Guardian* 30 March. London

Reason, Matthew (2006a) Young Audience and Live Theatre, Part 1: Methods, participation and memory in audience research. *Studies in Theatre and Performance*, 26 (2) 129-145

Reason, Matthew (2006b) Young Audience and Live Theatre, Part 2: Perceptions of liveness in performance. *Studies in Theatre and Performance,* 26 (3) 221-241

Reason, Matthew (2008) Thinking Theatre: Enhancing Children's Theatrical Experiences Through Philosophical Enquiry. *Childhood and Philosophy,* 4 (7). Available: www.filoeduc.org/childphilo/n7/Matthew_Reason.pdf

Reekie, Tony (2005) Revival of Theatre in Scotland: The Cinderella Story of Scottish Children's Theatre. In Bennett, S (ed) *Theatre for Children and Young People*. London, Aurora Metro Press

Ring, Kathy and Anning, Angela (2004) *Early Childhood Narratives Through Drawing*. TRACEY: Contemporary Drawing Research

Robinson, Ken (2001) *All Our Futures: Creativity, culture and education*. London, National Advisory Committee on Creative and Cultural Education

Roland, Craig (2007) Q*uestions to Ask Kids about Works of Art.* Art Junction, University of Florida

Rose, Jacqueline (1984) *The Case of Peter Pan, or, The Impossibility of Children's Fiction,* London, Macmillan

Sartre, Jean-Paul (1976) The Author, The Play and The Audience. In Contat, M and Rybalka, M (eds) *Sartre on Theatre.* London, Quartet Books

Sauter, Willmar (2000) *The Theatrical Event: Dynamics of performance and perception,* Iowa City, University of Iowa Press

Saywitz, Karen J (2002) Developmental Underpinnings of Children's Testimony. IN Westcott, H L, Davies, G M and Bull, R H (eds) *Children's Testimony: A handbook of psychological research and forensic practice.* Chichester, Wiley

Schoenmakers, Henri (1990) The Spectator in the Leading Role: Developments in reception and audience research within theatre studies. In Sauter, W (ed) *New Directions in Theatre Research.* Munksgaard, Nordic Theatre Studies 93-106

Schonmann, Shifra (2006) *Theatre as a Medium for Children and Young People: Images and observations,* Dordrecht, Springer

Scottish Arts Council (2006) *Theatre Style: Children's Theatre.* Available: www.scottisharts.org.uk

Shershow, Scott Cutler (1995) *Puppets and 'Popular' Culture,* Ithaca, Cornell University Press

Silverman, David (1993) *Interpreting Qualitative Data: Methods for analysing talk, text and interaction,* London, Sage

Smith, Ian (2007) *Asking Better Questions,* Paisley, Learning Unlimited

Sontag, Susan (1967) *Against Interpretation,* London, Eyre and Spottiswoode

Stavenhagen, Rodolfo (1998) Cultural Rights: A social science perspective. In Unesco (ed) *Cultural Rights and Wrongs.* Paris, UNESCO Publishing and Institute of Art and Law

Swortzell, Lowell (1993) Trying to like TiE: An American critic hopes TiE can be saved. In Jackson, T (ed) *Learning Through Theatre: New perspectives on Theatre in Education.* London, Routledge

Taunton, Martha (1983) Questioning Strategies to Encourage Young Children to Talk about Art. *Art Education,* 36 (4) 40-3

The Herald (2005) Dramatic Response over School Trips to the Theatre. *The Herald* 5 July. Glasgow

Tillis, Steve (1992) *Towards an Aesthetics of the Puppet,* Westport CT, Greenwood Press

Tulloch, John (2000) Approaching Theatre Audiences: Active school students and commoditised high culture. *Contemporary Theatre Review,* 10 (2) 85-104

Ubersfeld, Anne (1982) The Pleasure of the Spectator. *Modern Drama,* 25 (1) 127-139

Vine, Chris (1993) TiE and the Theatre of the Oppressed. In Jackson, T (ed) *Learning Through Theatre: New perspectives on Theatre in Education.* London, Routledge

Wilson, Graeme, Macdonald, Raymond, Byrne, Charles, Ewing, Sandra and Sheridan, Marion (2005) *Delivering the Arts in Scottish Schools.* Edinburgh, Scottish Exectuive Education Department

Wood, David (2005) Twenty-Five Years on Whirligig. In Bennett, S (ed) *Theatre for Children and Young People.* Aurora Metro Press

Young Scot (2004) *Expressing Themselves: National youth consultation on the arts.* Edinburgh, Young Scot and Scottish Arts Council

Index